Parents and Textbooks

Parents and Textbooks

Answers that Reveal Essential Steps for Improvement

Gerard Giordano

ROWMAN & LITTLEFIELD
Lanham • Boulder • New York • London

Published by Rowman & Littlefield
An imprint of The Rowman & Littlefield Publishing Group, Inc.
4501 Forbes Boulevard, Suite 200, Lanham, Maryland 20706
www.rowman.com

6 Tinworth Street, London SE11 5AL, United Kingdom

Copyright © 2019 by Gerard Giordano

All rights reserved. No part of this book may be reproduced in any form or by any electronic or mechanical means, including information storage and retrieval systems, without written permission from the publisher, except by a reviewer who may quote passages in a review.

British Library Cataloguing in Publication Information Available

Library of Congress Cataloging-in-Publication Data Available

ISBN: 978-1-4758-3896-1 (cloth : alk. paper)
ISBN: 978-1-4758-3897-8 (pbk. : alk. paper)
ISBN: 978-1-4758-3898-5 (electronic)

∞™ The paper used in this publication meets the minimum requirements of American National Standard for Information Sciences—Permanence of Paper for Printed Library Materials, ANSI/NISO Z39.48-1992.

Printed in the United States of America

This book highlights classroom conversations with my students.
Without their wit, insight, morality, and sensitivity,
it could not have been written.

Contents

List of Tables	ix
Preface: Who Has the Right Idea about Textbooks?	xiii
Acknowledgment	xv
1 Do Authors Have the Right Idea about Textbooks?	1
2 Do Californians Have the Right Idea about Textbooks?	11
3 Do Texans Have the Right Idea about Textbooks?	21
4 Do Marketers Have the Right Idea about Textbooks?	31
5 Do New Yorkers Have the Right Idea about Textbooks?	39
6 Do Publishers Have the Right Idea about Textbooks?	47
7 Do Parents Have the Right Idea about Textbooks?	55
8 Do Floridians Have the Right Idea about Textbooks?	63
9 Do Superintendents Have the Right Idea about Textbooks?	73
10 Do Journalists Have the Right Idea about Textbooks?	83
References	91
About the Author	111

List of Tables

1.1	Engineers Encourage Drivers to Operate Sophisticated Cars with Discretion	7
1.2	Engineers Encourage Drivers to Rely Completely on Sophisticated Cars	7
1.3	Authors Encourage Teachers to Use Sophisticated Textbooks with Discretion	8
1.4	Authors Encourage Teachers to Rely Completely on Sophisticated Textbooks	8
2.1	Federal Personnel Use Lax Guidelines to Identify Biased Trademarks	17
2.2	Federal Personnel Use Stringent Guidelines to Identify Biased Trademarks	18
2.3	California Legislators Use Lax Guidelines to Identify Biased Textbooks	18
2.4	California Legislators Use Stringent Guidelines to Identify Biased Textbooks	19
3.1	Judges Ask the Scientific Community to Approve Expert Witnesses	28
3.2	Judges Approve Expert Witnesses on Their Own	28
3.3	Texas Legislators Ask the SBOE to Select Textbooks	29
3.4	Texas Legislators Allow Local School Districts to Select Textbooks on Their Own	29

4.1	Marketers Assure Political Clients That They Will Benefit from Positive Publicity	36
4.2	Marketers Notice That Some Clients Benefit from Negative Publicity	37
4.3	Marketers Assure Textbook Publishers That They Will Benefit from Positive Publicity	37
4.4	Marketers Notice That Some Publishers Benefit from Negative Publicity	38
5.1	Cabinet Nominees Provide Straightforward Answers	43
5.2	A Nominee Provides Robotic Answers	44
5.3	Commissioners of Education Provide Straightforward Answers	44
5.4	A Commissioner Provides Robotic Answers	45
6.1	Publishers Hike Journal Prices	52
6.2	Publishers Control Journal Prices with Author-Paid Fees	52
6.3	Publishers Hike Textbook Prices	53
6.4	Publishers Control Textbook Prices with Bundled Purchasing Discounts	53
7.1	University Presidents Implement Trigger Warnings	60
7.2	A University President Refuses to Implement Trigger Warnings	61
7.3	Florida's Legislators Appoint Parents to State Textbook Committees	61
7.4	Florida's Legislators Disband State Textbook Committees	62
8.1	Florida's Legislators Strictly Regulate Liquor Sales	69
8.2	Legislators Pledge to Loosen Liquor Sales Regulations	70
8.3	Florida's Governors Loosely Regulate Textbook Purchases	70
8.4	A Governor Pledges to Tighten Textbook Purchasing Regulations	71
9.1	Auto Dealers Provide Precise Sales Reports	79
9.2	Dealers Provide Less Precise Sales Reports	79
9.3	A Florida Superintendent Provides Precise Reports about Textbook Purchasing	80

9.4	The Superintendent Provides Less Precise Reports about Textbook Purchasing	80
10.1	A University President Makes Controversial Recommendations	88
10.2	The President Reaches Out for Allies	89
10.3	Textbook Publishers Make Controversial Recommendations	89
10.4	The Publishers Reach Out for Allies	90

Preface

Who Has the Right Idea about Textbooks?

Great teachers . . . never do without textbooks. —Rabbi Seymour Rossel, quoted in "Why Textbooks," 2009

[Textbooks] can affect achievement as profoundly as teachers. —Science journalist Gina Kolata, 2013

[Textbooks are] crucial for students. —High school teacher Michael Zwaagstra, 2014

The absence of [textbooks is] unsettling. —Unidentified teacher, quoted in Boarding School Beak, 2014

Parents wanted to know what was transpiring at school. Needless to say, they asked their children. However, they did not have complete confidence in them: they knew that they could be distracted, daydreaming, or bored at school.

The parents also questioned teachers. But they did not have complete confidence in them, either. They feared that teachers would suppress important information if it could jeopardize their jobs.

The parents questioned principals, superintendents, and school board members. In every instance, the parents suspected that all had conflicts of interest.

The parents eventually asked politicians for their help. The politicians replied that they shared the parents' interest in scholastic information. Furthermore, they had a sure way to get it.

The politicians were going to rely on tests. However, the tests had to come from commercial publishers, whom they believed would be more objective than the educators.

Some parents were initially enthusiastic about commercial tests. They later changed their minds after they discovered how expensive and disruptive the tests were (Giordano, 2016).

The parents were disappointed by all of the groups from which they had requested assistance. Nonetheless, they still wanted essential scholastic information. They therefore resolved to search for it on their own.

The parents were unsure where to start their search. Some of them looked to the past for ideas.

The parents discovered that textbooks had once been considered the primary source for information about what was going on in classrooms. This made sense during eras when these materials were viewed as the foundation for instruction and learning.

The parents believed that textbooks were as critical today as they had been in the past. They decided to examine them thoroughly.

This book, which was inspired by parents, is part of a series about the questions that they posed about schools. Previous books have concentrated on their queries about teachers, educational administrators, tests, and students. This one concentrates on textbooks.

This book is intended for parents. However, it also is for the teachers, guidance counselors, principals, and superintendents who work in the schools. Finally, it is for college students who are preparing for careers in the schools, politicians who fund the schools, and businesspeople who create products for them.

Acknowledgment

Each of my books bears the indelible impression of my editor—Tom Koerner. I would have been lost without his creativity and vision.

Chapter One

Do Authors Have the Right Idea about Textbooks?

[Authors create] the textbooks . . . that drive instruction. —Journalist Stephanie Simon, 2015

[Textbook authors] . . . do not drive instruction [in this district]. —Katy Independent School District, 2016

I can think of nothing less professional than allowing [the authors of] a textbook to drive the curriculum. —Public school technology director Doug Johnson, 2015

We don't typically use the textbook to drive the curriculum in this district. —Public school curriculum director Margaret Pfaff, quoted by Davis, 2014

Automotive engineers hoped that technologically advanced vehicles would impress consumers. They claimed that the vehicles eventually had become so sophisticated that they could function on their own. Textbook authors made comparable claims about sophisticated scholastic materials.

SOPHISTICATED CARS

Automotive engineers kept an eye on vehicles from competing firms. They were particularly interested in those with new technology.

The engineers took note of innovative technology that regulated speed, engine revolutions, coolant temperature, braking distance, and fuel consumption. They made sure to place comparable technology into their own vehicles (Bishop, 2005; Rothfeder, 2014).

Enthusiasts

The engineers were proud of the computerized technology in their cars. They initially claimed that drivers could use it to assist them in driving. However, the engineers later claimed that they could trust it to operate their vehicles autonomously (Bizon, Dascalescu, & Mahdavi, 2014; Eskandarian, 2012).

Some of the engineers made even more startling claims. Those at Tesla Motors boasted that computer-monitored vehicles had a "view of the world that a driver alone cannot access, seeing in every direction simultaneously and on wavelengths that go far beyond the human senses" (Tesla Motors spokesperson, quoted by Lambert, 2016).

The engineers stated that computer-operated cars were not only self-driving but also safe-driving. They insisted that that these cars could safely stay within posted speed limits, change from one lane to another, maneuver around roadway obstacles, adapt to bad weather, and arrive at precise destinations. They concluded that these vehicles functioned "at a safety level substantially greater than that of a human driver" (Tesla Motors spokesperson, quoted by Lambert, 2016).

After automobile dealers had been supplied with self-driving cars, they had to identify the customers to whom they would sell them. They calculated that they would have their greatest success with individuals who were old or disabled (Dudley, 2014/2015; Fung, 2014; Hedli, 2014; National Council on Disability, 2015; Ramsey, Inada, & Kubota, 2016).

The dealers identified the owners of taxi businesses as another group that would be interested in self-driving cars. Taxi businesses noted that they currently were employing numerous operators. The dealers assured them that self-driving cars would eliminate the need for those operators (McFarland, 2017).

Skeptics

Some consumers doubted that self-driving cars were truly safe. Even some engineers had doubts. A small group of Tesla engineers worried about the vehicles from their own product line (Auric, 2017; Boudette, 2016; Dugan & Spector, 2017).

The skeptics had a stark message for persons who purchased self-driving cars: Always be alert. They explained that consumers might have to assume control of their vehicles at any moment (Hamers, 2016; Higgins & Colias, 2017; Mims, 2016).

Some skeptics even disapproved of the advertisements for self-driving cars. They believed that the ads encouraged people to take unreasonable risks (Keogh, 2016; Mims, 2016).

The owners of taxi businesses had been targeted as consumers. However, they were concerned about the higher prices of the self-driving vehicles.

Although they had been told that they would save enough money from insurance and driver salaries to compensate for this pricing difference, they still had doubts. Most of them were not ready to invest in the new cars (Korosec, 2016).

Some financial analysts worried about the long-term and indirect effects of self-driving cars. They feared that these effects might lead to unemployment, unstable financial markets, and a damaged economy (McFarland, 2017; Preston, 2016).

SOPHISTICATED TEXTBOOKS

When authors were preparing to write books, they considered the publishing opportunities available to them. They noted that these opportunities clustered into three categories: fiction books, nonfiction books, and textbooks.

Many authors were interested in fiction books. They knew that fiction books could be developed on a tight schedule, required relatively little effort, and had the potential to generate huge profits.

Authors were interested in nonfiction books. They knew that these books would take a substantial amount of time and effort to research. Nonetheless, they still were intrigued by their exceptionally long print histories.

The authors also were interested in textbooks. They knew that textbooks could take a great deal of time and effort to develop. However, they noted that textbooks remained in print for a decade or even longer.

A small group of authors had begun to write textbooks during the 1800s. They surprised everyone with the money that they made from them. They inspired colleagues to try their hand at writing textbooks.

The early textbook authors wished to produce materials that would genuinely entice consumers. They therefore examined the best-selling items of their era. All of them were struck by the textbooks that William McGuffey was writing during the middle and late 1800s.

McGuffey designed textbooks to help children read. However, he also designed them to help children lead moral lives: he packed them with Christian hymns, prayers, and homilies. He believed that these religious features would have an influence on the children who learned from the books as well as the adults who purchased them.

McGuffey made his books patriotic. He included nationalistic narratives and political speeches within them. He judged that these features would promote good citizenship and sales.

McGuffey placed exquisite illustrations in his textbooks. He was certain that they would stimulate student learning and sales (Gorn, 1998).

McGuffey had used religious content, patriotic passages, and lavish illustrations to make his books stand out. However, he was not finished. He had still more innovative features in mind. For example, he made sure that the academic skills within each book complemented those from the preceding book in his series.

McGuffey designed reading books with still another innovative academic feature: advice to teachers. He gave them suggestions about how to help students identify words, comprehend stories, and use pictorial cues.

McGuffey made sure that his books had academic aids for the students as well as their teachers. He supplied the students with vocabulary lists, definitions, specially highlighted concepts, summaries, glossaries, and homework assignments (Giordano, 2000).

The authors from rival publishing firms were impressed by McGuffey. They attributed his success to the religious material, patriotic passages, and alluring illustrations in his textbooks. They introduced similar features into their own books.

Although the authors at rival firms were impressed by the content that McGuffey had placed in his readers, they were equally impressed by the academic features he had placed in them. They especially admired the manner in which he sequenced skills, gave practical advice to teachers, and provided aids for students. Convinced that all these features had propelled sales, they incorporated them into their own books (Gorn, 1998).

Rivals noted that McGuffey had made one more extremely important contribution to textbook writing. He initially had advised teachers to use his textbooks with discretion. However, he later claimed that his books had become so sophisticated that they were virtually self-instructing. The competition believed that this claim had an enormous impact on consumers. They made the same claim about their own textbooks.

Enthusiasts

The early textbook authors pitched their materials to teachers. They assured them that their textbooks were filled with the curricular and instructional aids that the teachers valued.

The authors also pitched their textbooks to parents. They assured the parents that sound textbooks minimized the damage from any poorly trained teachers that their children encountered (Britton, Woodward, & Binkley, 2012).

Later authors came up with an additional reason to purchase textbooks. For example, they stated that the textbooks complemented standardized tests.

Two twenty-first-century presidents had made many people anxious about standardized tests. George W. Bush had raised anxiety when he set tests as the foundation for national educational policy. Obama increased this anxiety when he vowed to replace the Bush-era tests with ones that were even more challenging—the Common Core tests (Giordano, 2016).

The textbook authors embraced the testing movement. They claimed that their textbooks, which were synchronized to popular tests, would help children get higher scores on those tests (Broussard, 2014; Clawson, 2015; Kamenetz, 2106; Simon, 2015).

Skeptics

Early teachers had only a modicum of professional training. As a result, they struggled to assemble curricula and instruct students. They were relieved when they had textbooks on which to rely.

Teachers eventually had access to better professional training. They were able to get it at normal schools, colleges, and universities. After they became more confident, they deliberated about all aspects of their classrooms, including their textbooks (Giordano, 2003, 2012b).

Some of the teachers were disgruntled with textbooks. They complained about the regimented manner in which the authors were structuring them. They also complained about some of the information with which they were packing them (Beechhold, 1971).

Although teachers complained about the information that the authors had packed into textbooks, they also complained about the information that was omitted. They concluded that both of these features had made the books biased. They worried that the books presented skewed perspectives on gender, race, ethnicity, and religion. They assumed that the content was affecting their students' social attitudes, cultural values, and general worldviews (Berlatsky, 2012; Giordano, 2003, 2009).

Teachers were particularly disturbed by biased information within history textbooks. Nonetheless, they could not always agree on the best way to fix these books. Some of them demanded that authors make their books more nationalistic; others gave the opposite recommendation (Giordano, 2004; Hutchins, 2011; Loewen, 1995, 2010; Schweikart & Allen, 2004).

Teachers who were disgruntled with textbooks continued to use them. However, they declared that they would use them to supplement rather than drive instruction (Giordano, 2004, 2007).

The disgruntled teachers were anxious after they made this declaration. They worried about the way that principals, superintendents, and school board members would react. They also worried about the way that parents would react (Lent, 2012; Walker, Bean, & Dillard, 2010).

The teachers were wise to be wary of the principals, superintendents, and school board members. These groups made it clear that they had more confidence in textbook authors than teachers. They reminded the teachers that textbooks would prepare students for rigorous exams.

Many parents also disagreed with the teachers' views on textbooks. They told them to listen to their school administrators and school board members, who, like the textbook authors, had the right idea about how to promote student learning.

POSING QUESTIONS ABOUT SOPHISTICATED PRODUCTS

The next section of this chapter contains four activities. The first two activities focus on technologically advanced cars; the last two activities concentrate on instructionally advanced textbooks.

As engineers were developing cars with advanced technology, they advised drivers to operate them with discretion. However, they later encouraged them to rely completely on the technology.

As authors developed textbooks with more advanced instructional features, they initially directed teachers to use them with discretion. They later encouraged them to rely completely on those features.

The activities at the end of this chapter, as well as those at the ends of subsequent chapters, assist readers who are going through this book on their own. They give them opportunities to simulate the case method, an approach to problem-solving that is popular in university classrooms.

When professors employ the case method, they require their students to simultaneously examine several problems. They are not surprised if the students initially don't detect any similarities among these problems. However, they use questions to help them discern how the solution to one problem can be the key to another.

Although the activities that follow are appropriate for readers who are progressing through this book on their own, they are equally appropriate for readers who are using it in university classrooms (Giordano, 2009, 2010, 2011, 2012b).

Activity 1.1

Engineers made cars that were increasingly sophisticated. However, they cautioned drivers to operate them with discretion. How did groups respond?

Table 1.1 identifies two groups: consumers who were shopping for autos and owners of taxi businesses.

Complete the table by indicating the ways in which the groups responded to the engineers. You can use symbols.

Use the symbol – if the groups expressed low confidence in them. Use the symbol ± for moderate confidence and the symbol + for high confidence. As a final step, explain the basis for the symbols that you selected.

You can rely on the information in this chapter, additional information, or the information cited in the references. If you are reading this chapter with colleagues, you can confer with them.

Table 1.1. Engineers Encourage Drivers to Operate Sophisticated Cars with Discretion

Groups	Response*	Explanation
Consumers		
Taxi Owners		

* – Low
± Moderate
+ High

Activity 1.2

The engineers eventually gave drivers different advice about sophisticated automobiles: they encouraged them to rely completely on them. How did the groups respond?

Table 1.2 identifies two groups: consumers who were shopping for autos and owners of taxi businesses.

Complete the table by indicating the ways in which the groups responded to the engineers. You can use symbols.

Use the symbol – if the groups expressed low confidence in them. Use the symbol ± for moderate confidence and the symbol + for high confidence. As a final step, explain the bases for the symbols that you selected.

Table 1.2. Engineers Encourage Drivers to Rely Completely on Sophisticated Cars

Groups	Response*	Explanation
Consumers		
Taxi Owners		

* – Low
± Moderate
+ High

Activity 1.3

Authors made textbooks that were increasingly sophisticated. However, they cautioned teachers to use them with discretion. How did the groups respond?

Table 1.3 identifies two groups: teachers and parents.

Complete the table by indicating the ways in which the groups responded to the authors. You can use symbols.

Use the symbol – if the groups expressed low confidence in them. Use the symbol ± for moderate confidence and the symbol + for high confidence. As a final step, explain the basis for the symbols that you selected.

Table 1.3. Authors Encourage Teachers to Use Sophisticated Textbooks with Discretion

Groups	Response*	Explanation
Teachers		
Parents		

* – Low
± Moderate
+ High

Activity 1.4

The authors eventually gave teachers different advice about sophisticated textbooks: they encouraged them to rely completely on them. How did the groups respond?

Table 1.4 identifies two groups: teachers and parents.

Complete the table by indicating the ways in which the groups responded to the authors. You can use symbols.

Use the symbol – if the groups expressed low confidence in them. Use the symbol ± for moderate confidence and the symbol + for high confidence. As a final step, explain the basis for the symbols that you selected.

Table 1.4. Authors Encourage Teachers to Rely Completely on Sophisticated Textbooks

Groups	Response*	Explanation
Teachers		
Parents		

* – Low
± Moderate
+ High

SUMMARY

Engineers created cars with increasingly sophisticated technology. Although they initially directed persons to use this technology as an aid while driving, they later told them to rely completely on it. As authors created textbooks with increasingly sophisticated instructional features, they advised teachers to rely completely on those features.

Chapter Two

Do Californians Have the Right Idea about Textbooks?

Textbook publishers . . . have to look at [California's textbook laws].
—Professor Don Romesburg, quoted by Morris, 2016

[Textbooks must not reflect] adversely upon persons because of their . . . occupation. —California State Law, quoted by Friedersdorf, 2015

Textbooks compatible with the new California curriculum laws should be systematically avoided. —Political commentator Stanley Kurtz, 2016

Politicians don't write good textbooks. —*Los Angeles Times* Editorial Board, 2011

Personnel at the federal patent and trademark were upset about biased trademarks. Legislators in California were upset about biased textbooks. Although both groups took corrective steps, they were surprised by the consequences.

BANNING BIASED TRADEMARKS

Staff members at the United States Patent and Trademark Office review applications for new trademarks. They make sure that they do not duplicate trademarks that already have been approved. They also make sure that they do not exhibit bias. If they judge that both standards are met, they authorize the trademark for a ten-year span.

When the office's staff members review applications for renewed trademarks, they use the same two standards as for initial trademarks. If they judge that both standards are met, they renew the trademarks.

Enthusiasts

During the Obama administration, staff members examined trademarks that had been awarded during earlier administrations. They detected numerous irregularities. They vowed to do a better job.

The staff wished to demonstrate that they were being fair to applicants during their new and more thorough deliberations. They therefore provided the applicants with precise guidelines. They even gave them examples of terms and images that would disqualify their requests. These examples pertained to race, ethnicity, religion, economic status, gender, and sexual orientation.

The staff members had confidence in their new guidelines. However, they needed a high-profile case to showcase their benefits.

The staff members were excited when a popular football team, the Washington Redskins, filed to renew its trademark. They believed that this was the case for which they had been waiting (Guillermo, 2016).

The owners of the Washington Redskins had obtained their first trademark during the 1930s. They had encountered no problems since that time. They did not expect any when they filed for renewal in 2014.

The owners had expected the staff of United States Patent and Trademark Office to approve their 2014 application. They were shocked when they did not. They demanded an explanation (Savage, 2016).

The staff members stated that that the application did not comply with their office's current guidelines. They explained that "redskins" was an offensive, demeaning, and racist term.

The staff members anticipated that the owners would complain. However, they had a retort ready for them: The new guidelines had been endorsed by President Obama himself. They hoped that this piece of information would settle the matter (Liptak, 2016, 2017; "Redskins, and Other Troubling Trademarks," 2016).

The football team owners were not satisfied. They contended that most persons, including American Indians, had no problem with their team's name.

The owners had their own theory about why the office staff had denied their request. They contended that they were trying to attract publicity for their new guidelines.

The staff members replied that they were not picking on the owners. They stated that they were going to stick by their original decision and deny their application. They added that they were going to treat all applications in a similar fashion ("Washington Redskins," 2016).

The owners vowed to raise an uproar over the decision. In fact, they were going to file suit over it (Cox, Clement, & Vargas, 2016).

Skeptics

The office staff had to deal with numerous low-profile trademark applications. They initially took little notice of an application from four Asian Americans.

The Asian Americans were rock musicians. They had given their band an attention-getting name—The Slants. They wished to trademark that name.

The staff turned down the application. They stated that the term "slants" was disparaging, offensive, and racist (Hananel, 2017).

The musicians explained that they were using the term "slants" ironically. They pleaded with the staff members to recognize that it was a critical element of a campaign against racism (Katyal, 2016; Tam, 2017).

The staff members stood by their ruling. In fact, they buttressed it with a fifty-page legal brief. They expected this document to silence the musicians.

The musicians were not intimidated by the legal papers. Quite to the contrary, they announced that they were going to sue the United States Patent and Trademark Office. They warned that they were ready to take their suit all the way to the Supreme Court (Savage, 2016).

The staff members had to deal with two suits—one from the football team and the other from the rock band. They initially were confident that they would win both. However, they became less confident after they saw the storm of publicity that the suits created.

The staff members worried how businesspeople would respond to the publicity. They realized that businesspeople were interested because of the trademark applications that they routinely submitted to their office.

As it turned out, businesspeople were troubled. They accused the staff members of imposing their own notions of polite language onto trademark applications. They warned the staff members to be careful of the damage that they could cause if they continued to follow this practice.

The members of the office's staff were genuinely concerned about how businesspeople were responding to the two legal cases. However, they also were concerned about how politicians were responding. They realized that the politicians would have to take public stances on the cases.

President Obama had supported the office's staff after the decision against the football team. He announced that he would continue to back them after the decision against the rock band (Savage, 2016).

Democratic politicians stood with their president. They stated that the new trademark guidelines were appropriate and long overdue. They encouraged federal personnel to keep them in place and rigorously enforce them (Farley, 2016).

Republican politicians sided with the disgruntled businesspeople. They stated that the guidelines were flagrantly intrusive. They urged the federal trademark personnel to back down from their confrontations with the football team and the rock band (Bhagwat, 2016).

The trademark personnel were interested in the reactions of businesspeople and politicians. However, they also were interested in those of the general public. They anticipated that this group's reaction would have a major influence on the courts (Coscarelli, 2017).

The trademark personnel investigated the number of persons who agreed with them in the football case. They felt sanguine after polls showed that a large segment of the public was in agreement. They then investigated the number of persons who agreed with them in the rock band case. They became nervous after they discovered that a much smaller group supported them.

BANNING BIASED TEXTBOOKS

California's legislators were responsible for the textbooks in their state's public schools. However, they routinely delegated this responsibility to their Board of Education.

The members of the State Board of Education resolved to approve only appropriate textbooks. They assumed that their commitment was apparent in the guidelines on which they relied.

The board members believed that their guidelines enabled them to make fair decisions about textbooks. They circulated them to constituents and publishers. They hoped that their constituents would signify approval. They hoped that the publishers would use them to customize textbooks.

The board members initially were enthusiastic about their textbook guidelines. They were sure that they reflected California's distinctive curricula. However, they later had doubts about them. They judged that they were extremely effective for identifying textbooks with curricular irregularities but less effective for identifying those with biases.

The board members created new guidelines. They made sure to single out textbooks with disparaging remarks about racial and ethnic groups. They then submitted the guidelines to their legislators for approval.

The state legislators heartily approved of the new guidelines. In fact, they shared them with colleagues from other states, encouraging them to replicate the new guidelines (Giordano, 2003).

Enthusiasts

California's legislators were pleased with their new textbook guidelines. They expected their constituents to be pleased as well. They were surprised when some of them expressed concerns.

The disgruntled constituents liked the way that the guidelines treated racial and ethnic biases. However, they did not think they had gone far enough: They believed that they should have addressed gender biases with equal rigor.

The legislators listened respectfully. They assured the disgruntled constituents that they would act on their advice. They passed a law to redress problems related to gender-biased textbooks. They stipulated that all textbooks had to exclude any gender-biased comments or images. They added that the textbooks should explicitly highlight current and historical contributions of both women and men.

The legislators believed they had satisfied their constituents. However, they soon were contacted by more people who wanted additional restrictions on textbooks. They explained that textbooks had failed to explicitly acknowledge the contributions of key racial and ethnic groups. They identified the groups they had in mind: Native Americans, African Americans, Mexican Americans, Asian Americans, Pacific Islanders, and some European Americans (Friedersdorf, 2015).

More constituents kept coming forward with concerns about textbooks. They identified additional problems: Textbooks had failed to underscore the explicit contributions of lesbian, gay, bisexual, and transgender Americans (Morris, 2016).

The legislators had listened to multiple groups. In each case, they had tried to appease them. They assumed that every group had conveyed its concerns. They therefore must have been shocked when still one more group approached them (Austin, 2016).

The members of this group complained that textbooks did not represent occupations appropriately. They contended that they had shown less respect for bus driving, grounds keeping, and hotel work than they had for engineering, medicine, and accounting. They demanded that they display equal respect for all occupations.

The legislators were ready to impose one more restriction on textbooks. They believed that it was a commonsense restriction. They stipulated that textbooks had to profess respect for diverse occupations. They did not supply a list of occupations: they intended the list to be all-inclusive (Friedersdorf, 2015).

Skeptics

The legislators were excited about the new textbooks that would appear in the schools. They believed that they would have educational benefits.

The legislators hoped that the new textbooks would have political as well as educational benefits. They assumed that they would have a positive impact on parents, a group on which they depended for votes (Kurtz, 2016; Mirengoff, 2016).

The parents served on the textbook selection committees at local schools. As a result, they had plentiful opportunities to review prospective books (e.g., Ontario-Montclair School District, 2014).

The parents were interested in how textbooks depicted their ancestral countries. For example, some of them, who were Indian American, wanted to see how history and social studies textbooks depicted India.

The Indian American parents wished to make sure that textbooks conveyed accurate information. They contended that they should use the term "South Asia" when referring to the region that comprised India, Pakistan, and Nepal. They also contended that the textbooks should contain maps depicting early as well as current national borders in the region (Medina, 2016).

After the Indian American parents had examined the textbooks, they documented the problems that they had detected. They then blamed the state's textbook guidelines for those problems. They explained that the guidelines had not given the publishers enough guidance.

Indian American parents were not the only group that detected problems. Filipino American, Korean American, and Mexican American parents bristled at the information that textbooks provided about their respective ancestral countries. Furthermore, they all were convinced that poorly crafted textbook guidelines were responsible for those problems. They demanded that the legislators change them.

Academic publishers were nervous whenever legislators became involved with textbooks. They worried that they would prescribe solutions that created more problems than they solved.

The publishers gave an example of a problem for which legislators had been partially responsible. They noted that the legislators continually were directing them to make eleventh-hour changes to the content in their books. However, they contended that this tinkering, which was intended to make the books more equitable, had also made them more expensive.

The publishers gave an example of another problem for which the legislators were responsible. They noted that they had banned textbooks with statements disparaging any occupation. However, they pointed out that their history books contained disparaging statements about nineteenth-century slave trading. They asked the legislators if they truly had intended to ban those books (Friedersdorf, 2015).

RESPONDING TO QUESTIONS ABOUT BIAS

The staff at the United States Patent and Trademark Office detected problems with biased trademarks. State legislators in California detected problems with biased textbooks. Both groups believed that stringent guidelines would eliminate the problems.

Activity 2.1

Staff members at the United States Patent and Trademark Office wished to eliminate biased trademarks. However, they historically had relied on relatively lax guidelines. How did the textbooks groups respond?

Table 2.1 identifies two groups: businesspeople who applied for trademarks and members of the public.

Complete the table by indicating the ways in which the groups responded to the staff. You can use symbols.

Use the symbol − if the groups expressed low confidence in them. Use the symbol ± for moderate confidence and the symbol + for high confidence. As a final step, explain the basis for the symbols that you selected.

You can rely on the information in this chapter, additional information, or the information cited in the references. If you are reading this chapter with colleagues, you can confer with them.

Table 2.1. Federal Personnel Use Lax Guidelines to Identify Biased Trademarks

Groups	Response*	Explanation
Businesspeople		
Public		

* − Low
± Moderate
+ High

Activity 2.2

Staff members at the United States Patent and Trademark Office pledged to do a better job of eliminating biased trademarks. They made their guidelines more stringent. How did the groups respond?

Table 2.2 identifies two groups: businesspeople who applied for trademarks and members of the public.

Complete the table by indicating the ways in which the groups responded to the staff. You can use symbols.

Use the symbol − if the groups expressed low confidence in them. Use the symbol ± for moderate confidence and the symbol + for high confidence. As a final step, explain the basis for the symbols that you selected.

Table 2.2. Federal Personnel Use Stringent Guidelines to Identify Biased Trademarks

Groups	Response*	Explanation
Businesspeople		
Public		

* − Low
± Moderate
\+ High

Activity 2.3

California legislators wished to eliminate biased textbooks. However, they historically had relied on relatively lax guidelines. How did groups respond?

Table 2.3 identifies two groups: textbook publishers and parents.

Complete the table by indicating the ways in which the groups responded to the legislators. You can use symbols.

Use the symbol − if the groups expressed low confidence in them. Use the symbol ± for moderate confidence and the symbol + for high confidence. As a final step, explain the basis for the symbols that you selected.

Table 2.3. California Legislators Use Lax Guidelines to Identify Biased Textbooks

Groups	Response*	Explanation
Publishers		
Parents		

* − Low
± Moderate
\+ High

Activity 2.4

California legislators pledged to do a better job of eliminating biased textbooks. They made their guidelines more stringent. How did the groups respond?

Table 2.4 identifies two groups: textbook publishers and parents.

Complete the table by indicating the ways in which the groups responded to the legislators. You can use symbols.

Use the symbol − if the groups expressed low confidence in them. Use the symbol ± for moderate confidence and the symbol + for high confidence. As a final step, explain the basis for the symbols that you selected.

Table 2.4. California Legislators Use Stringent Guidelines to Identify Biased Textbooks

Groups	Response*	Explanation
Publishers		
Parents		

* − Low
± Moderate
\+ High

SUMMARY

The staff at the United States Patent and Trademark Office was troubled by biased trademarks. State legislators in California were troubled by biased textbooks. Both groups created stringent guidelines to solve their problems. Both groups were surprised by the results.

Chapter Three

Do Texans Have the Right Idea about Textbooks?

[This committee is responsible for] adopting instructional materials. —Texas State Board of Education, 2017

[The Texas State Board of Education] has statutory obligations to promote patriotism [in textbooks]. —Publisher Cynthia Dunbar, quoted by DeCourcey, 2016

Right-wing board members . . . impose their own religious and political beliefs [on textbooks]. —Texas State Teachers Association president Rita Haecker, quoted by Walker, 2016

[The Texas State Board of Education routinely requires textbook publishers] to make hundreds of last-minute edits. —Journalist Will Weissert, 2014

Judges had to decide whether expert witnesses could testify in court. State legislators had to decide whether textbooks could be used in school. Both groups initially delegated these responsibilities. However, they later changed their minds.

REGULATING COURTROOM TESTIMONY

R. W. Brown was an early twentieth-century physician in the District of Columbia. He was one of the few African Americans practicing medicine in that community.

Brown's two adult daughters lived with him. They never doubted their father's devotion to his patients. They could not help but be impressed that he would meet with his patients in their home at all hours.

The daughters were startled one night by a loud noise coming from their father's office. When they ran to investigate, they found their father on the floor, a pistol by his side, and a bullet in his temple. They called the police for help.

The police arrived, examined the corpse, combed the office, and interviewed neighbors. They concluded that Brown had been murdered.

Brown was an esteemed and beloved resident of the community. The police were under pressure to locate the person who had killed him. However, they did not have a witness, a suspect, or even a lead.

The police appealed to community members. They told them that Brown's daughters would pay a $1,000 reward for information about the assailant. They fretted when no one came forward.

For six months, the police did not make any progress. However, they then suddenly scheduled a press conference. At it, they revealed that they had found the murderer.

The police credited two detectives for solving the crime. The detectives explained that they had been questioning a local man about some burglaries. They claimed that this man, James Frye, had spontaneously brought up Brown's murder, admitted that he was the assailant, and signed a confession.

Although Frye had confessed, he still had to stand trial. During his arraignment, he told the judge that he could not afford an attorney. He requested a public defender.

Two public defenders were assigned to Frye. These men took a genuine interest in him. They asked him what truly had transpired. They especially wanted to hear the details surrounding his confession.

Frye stated that the two detectives had tricked him into making the confession. He explained that they had promised him that he would go to trial but be found innocent and released. He expected to then be given a share of the reward the detectives would have collected (*Frye v. U.S.*, 2017).

The defense lawyers believed Frye's story. Nonetheless, they worried that he would be convicted because of his jailhouse confession. They needed a way to undermine the court's confidence in that confession. They went to Professor William Marston for assistance.

Marston was a psychologist who had invented a machine to detect lies. He would strap persons to it, pose questions to them, and record their blood pressure. He stated that elevated blood pressure indicated that the respondents were telling lies while flat pressure indicated that they were telling the truth (Bunn, 2012).

Marston connected Frye to his machine, quizzed him about the crime, and kept a record of his blood pressure. After analyzing the results, he concluded that Frye was innocent.

The defense attorneys realized that Marston was critical to their case. They requested permission to call him as an expert witness.

The prosecutor objected. He characterized Marston as a crackpot psychologist and his lie detector as pseudoscientific junk.

The judge listened patiently to the public defenders and the prosecutor. He then acknowledged that he did not know enough about psychological research to rule on the request. He asked how members of the scientific community viewed Marston's work.

The defense lawyers were nervous. They admitted that Marston's fellow scientists were skeptical of his research. However, they noted that the research was still new. They asked the judge to consider this limitation when he made his decision.

Enthusiasts

The defense lawyers waited for the judge's decision. They were upset when they heard it: Marston was barred from the trial.

Judges throughout the country quickly learned about the ruling. They were interested in it because they regularly had to decide whether expert witnesses could testify in their own courtrooms. They were convinced that they should use the precedent set in the Fry case: They should determine whether witnesses would be presenting evidence that was generally accepted by the scientific community.

The new criterion was initially referred to as the *General-Acceptance Standard*. However, it commonly was identified as the *Frye Standard*.

Defense attorneys were nervous when judges invoked the Frye Standard. They worried that they were using it to exclude witnesses simply because they had relied on innovative investigative tools.

The judges were in a bind. They needed to present a rejoinder to the defense attorneys. They eventually devised one. They conceded that attorneys should be able to call expert witnesses who relied on innovative investigative procedures. They therefore agreed to personally make decisions about whether these witnesses could testify. However, they needed a new criterion on which to base their decisions.

The judges developed the new criterion during the 1970s. They showcased it during a prominent case: *Daubert v. Merrell Dow Pharmaceuticals*. Because of its connection to this case, the new criterion became known as the *Daubert Standard*.

Judges who used the Daubert Standard would ask the attorneys whether prospective expert witnesses had gathered evidence with reputable scientific

24   Chapter Three

techniques. They wanted to know if they had conducted experiments, set up control groups, compensated for extraneous variables, calculated error rates, and relied on credible scientific theories. After they had listened to their responses, they would rule on whether the witnesses could testify (Roberts, DeCandio, & Ingersoll, 2017).

Skeptics

Judges had been disconcerted when defense attorneys complained about the Frye Standard. They hoped that they would be satisfied by the Daubert Standard.

Defense attorneys were initially excited about the Daubert Standard. However, they eventually changed their minds (Smith, 2000).

When defense attorneys were getting ready to call expert witnesses, they would brief them about the Daubert Standard. They told them to contend that their testimony was based on scientifically gathered evidence. However, they were distressed when prosecutors hired their own expert witnesses to challenge these contentions. They concluded that the new standard could be just as troublesome as the previous one (Lewis, 2014; Morgenstern, 2016).

REGULATING TEXTBOOKS

The members of the Texas Senate and the Texas Senate House of Representatives were accountable for public education. They historically had delegated many of their responsibilities to the State Board of Education (SBOE).

Fifteen persons served on Texas's SBOE. Although they may have been a small group, they made decisions with huge consequences. Their decisions influenced every school and community in the state (State Board of Education, 2017).

The board members regularly dealt with controversial issues. As a result, they were used to drawing attention. However, they attracted their greatest attention when they were making decisions about textbooks (Texas Education Agency, 2017).

The board members knew that their constituents cared about textbooks. They were struck by the passionate comments that they made about them. They weighed those comments when they made decisions about whether to approve textbooks for the schools.

The board members kept a list of the textbooks that they had approved. They adjured school administrators to pay close attention to it.

Enthusiasts

The school administrators did pay attention to Texas's list of approved textbooks. They realized that they could use their state-allocated textbook funds only for materials that were on this list.

Some of the school administrators were resentful of the list. They pointed out that it limited their access to textbooks. However, others valued the list because it shielded them from making unpopular decisions about controversial textbooks.

The executives at publishing companies also paid attention to the list of approved textbooks. They realized that Texas was one of the largest textbook markets in the country. They designed their products so that they would be added to the list. Those who were successful were pleased (Wray, 2015).

Members of the public were another group that paid attention to the list of approved textbooks. They wanted to make sure that it contained books that embodied their values and attitudes. Those who approved of the textbooks on the list were pleased.

Skeptics

Texas legislators had made the SBOE responsible for textbooks. They watched as this board then created a list of approved textbooks. They were generally pleased with it. However, they still wished to determine how different groups were reacting to it.

The legislators heard abundant criticism about the list. They noted that much of it came from journalists.

Many of the journalists were not pleased with the list. Even those who did not reside in Texas complained about it. They claimed that the books on the list were winding up in the classrooms of their respective states. They contended that these books were inappropriate because they overemphasized topics such as American exceptionalism, free-market economic principles, and politically conservative ideology (Gewertz, 2015; Isensee, 2015; Thevenot, 2010).

The journalists had advice about how to improve the textbooks selection process. They directed the legislators to exclude the SBOE from this process (Blake, 2010; Collier & Cobler, 2015; Jervis, 2014; Ramirez, 2016; Smith, 2014).

The legislators were not particularly disconcerted by the journalists. They suspected that many of them, especially those who represented national media organizations, had political motives for discrediting Texas. They were ready to ignore their criticism and discard their advice.

The legislators also heard criticism from the parents in their state. In this case, they were extremely solicitous. They listened attentively to them.

The parents contended that textbooks on the state list had problems. However, they disagreed among themselves about the precise nature of those problems. Some of them alleged that the books were politically too conservative; others alleged that they were not sufficiently conservative. In spite of their differences, they all agreed on one important point: The SBOE had no business selecting their children's textbooks (DeCiccio, 2013; DeCourcey, 2016; "Texas Textbooks," 2010).

The legislators also listened to school administrators. They discovered that they were another group with strong views about the textbooks on the state list.

Many of the school administrators were dissatisfied with the textbooks. They urged the legislators to change the current selection procedures. They gave them the same recommendation that the parents had given them: Exclude the SBOE from the procedures (Tuma, 2016).

The school administrators were convinced that they would need help to change the minds of their legislators. They pleaded with their professional organization, the Texas Association of School Administrators (TASA), to get involved.

The leaders of the TASA did get involved. They were eager to strip the SBOE of its textbook authority. They were joined by the leaders of several other high-profile educational organizations, including the Texas Computer Education Association (Nagel, 2009).

Publishers were another group that had been complaining about the SBOE. They were upset when it mandated costly textbook changes. They were even more upset when it later refused to approve the books to which they had made these changes (Blue, 2014).

The publishers urged the legislators to remove the SBOE's textbook authority. They persuaded several powerful business associations to help lobby them ("Dear Texas Lawmaker," 2009; "Texas Approves," 2014).

The Texas legislators had delegated their textbook responsibilities to the SBOE. After investigating how it was handling them, they concluded that it was needlessly arousing parents, educators, businesspeople, and journalists. They wished to mollify the disgruntled constituents.

The legislators believed that they had a way to suppress the tumult. They noted that school districts could spend state funds only on SBOE-approved materials. They introduced a bill authorizing them to spend those funds on non-SBOE-approved materials ("Actions of the 82nd Legislature," 2017; Nagel, 2009).

Although the legislators were ready to introduce their bill, they anticipated that it would be extremely controversial. They therefore wished to draw attention away from the bill's primary purpose, which was to remove the SBOE from the textbook-approval process. They gave it a misleading name: the Ed Tech Choice Bill (Nagel, 2009).

Some Texans did not support the Ed Tech Choice Bill. Needless to say, members of the SBOE did not. They realized that it would prevent them from making important decisions about classroom materials.

The board members intended to block the Ed Tech Choice Bill. However, they were not sure that they would succeed. They therefore hatched a backup plan. They decided that they would maintain their list of approved textbooks, even if that list was no longer mandatory. They predicted that their list still would be used by those school administrators who were too timid to choose books on their own (State Board of Education, 2017).

RESPONDING TO QUESTIONS ABOUT DECISION-MAKING

Judges had to decide which expert witnesses could testify in court. Although they initially delegated this responsibility to scientists, they later made the decisions on their own.

Texas legislators had to decide which textbooks school districts could purchase. Although they initially delegated this responsibility to the SBOE, they later allowed individual school districts to make the decisions on their own.

Activity 3.1

Judges had to decide whether to approve expert witnesses for trials. They historically had delegated this responsibility to the scientific community. How did groups respond?

Table 3.1 identifies two groups: prosecuting attorneys and defense attorneys.

Complete the table by indicating the ways in which the groups responded to the judges. You can use symbols.

Use the symbol – if the groups expressed low confidence in them. Use the symbol ± for moderate confidence and the symbol + for high confidence. As a final step, explain the basis for the symbols that you selected.

You can rely on the information in this chapter, additional information, or the information cited in the references. If you are reading this chapter with colleagues, you can confer with them.

Table 3.1. Judges Ask the Scientific Community to Approve Expert Witnesses

Groups	Response*	Explanation
Prosecuting Attorneys		
Defense Attorneys		

* – Low
± Moderate
+ High

Activity 3.2

Judges were pressured to find an alternative way of approving expert witnesses. They began to approve them on their own. How did the groups respond?

Table 3.2 identifies two groups: prosecuting attorneys and defense attorneys.

Complete the table by indicating the ways in which the groups responded to the judges. You can use symbols.

Use the symbol – if the groups expressed low confidence in them. Use the symbol ± for moderate confidence and the symbol + for high confidence. As a final step, explain the basis for the symbols that you selected.

Table 3.2. Judges Approve Expert Witnesses on Their Own

Groups	Response*	Explanation
Prosecuting Attorneys		
Defense Attorneys		

* – Low
± Moderate
+ High

Activity 3.3

Texas legislators had to select the textbooks that school districts could purchase with state funds. They historically had delegated this responsibility to the State Board of Education. How did groups respond?

Table 3.3 identifies two groups: textbook publishers and parents.

Complete the table by indicating the ways in which the groups responded to the legislators. You can use symbols.

Use the symbol – if the groups expressed low confidence in them. Use the symbol ± for moderate confidence and the symbol + for high confidence. As a final step, explain the basis for the symbols that you selected.

Table 3.3. Texas Legislators Ask the SBOE to Select Textbooks

Groups	Response*	Explanation
Publishers		
Parents		

* – Low
  ± Moderate
  + High

Activity 3.4

Texas legislators were pressured to find an alternative way of selecting textbooks. They allowed the individual school districts to select them on their own. How did the groups respond?

Table 3.4 identifies two groups: textbook publishers and parents.

Complete the table by indicating the ways in which the groups responded to the legislators. You can use symbols.

Use the symbol – if the groups expressed low confidence in them. Use the symbol ± for moderate confidence and the symbol + for high confidence. As a final step, explain the basis for the symbols that you selected.

Table 3.4. Texas Legislators Allow Local School Districts to Select Textbooks on Their Own

Groups	Response*	Explanation
Publishers		
Parents		

* – Low
  ± Moderate
  + High

SUMMARY

Judges had to decide whether expert witnesses could testify in courtrooms. Texas legislators had to decide whether textbooks could be used in public schools. Both groups initially delegated these responsibilities. However, they later changed their minds.

Chapter Four

Do Marketers Have the Right Idea about Textbooks?

Why must my children's school bags be so heavy? —Parent Harry Wallop, 2014

My daughter's school backpack got so heavy [because of the thick textbooks in it]. —Parent Tara Parker-Pope, 2015

[Textbook-filled] backpacks spell chronic back pain. —Health columnist Jane Brody, 2012

[This office is imposing] maximum weight standards for elementary and secondary school textbooks. —California Department of Education, 2016

Marketers believed that politicians would be harmed by negative publicity. They therefore advised them to avoid it. They gave the same advice to textbook publishers. However, they later found instances in which both groups had benefited from negative publicity.

PROMOTING POLITICIANS

Marketers promoted commercial products through advertising. They experimented with two different approaches.

The marketers wrote the textual scripts of ads. They then placed those ads where persons would see them. After observing the results, they concluded that the ads were highly effective (Chaffey, 2012).

The marketers experimented with a different type of advertising. They established websites on which consumers made comments about their clients' products. These comments on the websites became de-facto ads. The marketers noted that this approach, because it relied on unedited comments, sometimes had extremely negative results (Newman, 2014).

The marketers were willing to arrange either type of ad. Nonetheless, they recommended the ads with scripted messages. They explained to their clients that the scripted ads allowed them to directly control the messages associated with their products.

The marketers were pleased by the success they had in retailing: They had helped clients attract consumers. They were convinced that they could have similar success in politics: They could help clients attract voters.

The marketers presented political clients with the same menu of services that they had presented to their business clients. They offered to arrange scripted or unscripted ads. However, they recommended that they rely exclusively on scripted ads. They added that these ads would be most effective if they were featured on broadcast television.

Politicians listened carefully to the marketers. Those who were running for president in the 2016 election were extremely interested. They asked how much they would have to budget for scripted television ads.

The marketers told the candidates that television advertising would be expensive. They estimated that each candidate would have to raise more than one hundred million dollars just for this type of publicity.

Enthusiasts

Jeb Bush was competing in the Republican primary election. He was very nervous because he was going up against numerous rivals in the early stages of the 2016 presidential campaign. When he asked marketers for advice, he was told to immediately start raising funds (Roberts, 2016).

The marketers were pleased when Bush quickly developed a huge money advantage over his rivals. They counseled him to spend it on television ads.

The marketers guaranteed Bush that he would win the primary elections on the basis of ads. They believed that he, therefore, should save his stamina for the general election.

Bush took the marketers' advice. He did not exhaust himself making personal appearances. He was convinced that ads would suffice.

Skeptics

Bush did not win the Republican primaries. He was shocked.

The marketers also were shocked. After all, they had predicted that Bush, because of his fund-raising prowess, would win. They had made the same prediction for Hillary Clinton, who had a huge fund-raising advantage in the Democratic primaries. Although they were mortified by Bush's loss, they felt vindicated by Clinton's victory.

The marketers regrouped for the general election, in which Clinton was running against Donald Trump. They were ready to once again forecast the results: They predicted that Clinton, who had paid for many more ads than Trump, would win.

Not everyone agreed with this forecast. Some persons were skeptical of it. Although the skeptics conceded that Trump had purchased few ads, they noted that he had generated an unprecedented amount of unpaid media coverage.

The skeptics referred to unpaid media coverage as "earned publicity." They were convinced that the marketers had underestimated it during the Republican primaries. They believed that they were underestimating it again during the general election (Confessore & Yourish, 2016; Rutenberg, 2016).

The marketers ignored the skeptics. They were confident that paid media ads would win the election. They noted that Trump's unpaid coverage, even though it was enormous, was almost exclusively negative. They were sure that it would be of little help to him (Friedman, 2016a, 2016b; Streiff, 2016).

PROMOTING TEXTBOOKS

Early publishers had wished to expand their product lines. Although many of them had contemplated adding textbooks, they held back. They worried that the market was not strong enough to justify the money that they would have to invest.

Those publishers who did not invest in textbooks were soon remorseful. They realized that the market was more robust and lucrative than they had ever imagined.

Enthusiasts

The early scholastic publishers hoped to create best-sellers. They therefore designed textbooks that would appeal to three key groups: school administrators, teachers, and parents. They believed that these groups determined whether their books would be purchased or not.

The teachers viewed textbooks as instructional tools. They were attracted to those that had features such as maps, charts, tables, diagrams, full-color pictorial images, chapter summaries, quizzes, and lists of key vocabulary words. They were not attracted to those that lacked these features (Giordano, 2003).

School administrators viewed textbooks from a different perspective than teachers: They considered them to be costly purchases. Because they had limited funds, they wanted the books to be durable. They preferred those with thick pages, sturdy covers, and reinforced bindings (Giordano, 2003).

After the publishers had listened to the teachers and school administrators, they went to the parents. The parents agreed with the teachers that textbooks should be packed with instructional aids. However, they also agreed with school administrators that they should be durable (Giordano, 2012a, 2015).

The publishers wished to be responsive to all three consumer groups. They stated that they would expand the new editions of their textbooks to include more pages with instructional aids. They promised that they also would make the books more durable than the current ones. However, they cautioned that these features would make the books larger and heavier.

After they had produced their new textbooks, the publishers wanted to publicize them. They hired marketers to assist them.

The marketers were eager to help. They described two ways to get publicity. They could arrange ads that comprised the unscripted testimonials of customers. Alternatively, they could showcase ads that they and their staffs had scripted (Jenkins, 2006).

The marketers did not think that the publishers should count on customer-supplied testimonials. They noted that the customers, although they might be eager to share their opinions, could make remarks that would hinder sales.

The marketers concluded that the publishers should rely exclusively on scripted ads. They encouraged publishers to highlight them in emails, flyers, and catalogs (Lusk, 2014).

Skeptics

The publishers took the marketers' advice and commissioned scripted ads. They assumed that teachers and school administrators were viewing them. They assumed that some parents were viewing them as well.

The parents were not impressed by the scripted textbook ads. They questioned whether they were accurate. They accused the publishers of holding back key information, such as details about the weight of the textbooks. They were convinced that the publishers had made their textbooks too hefty for children to handle safely (Monahan, 2015).

The parents noted that their children carried the heavy textbooks in their backpacks. They contacted medical professionals, who attested to the skeletal and muscular damage that the children were sustaining. The parents also contacted journalists, who began to broadcast this information to a wide audience (Brody, 2012; "Problem Backpacks," 2017; Wallop, 2014).

The parents had formed an alliance with medical professionals and journalists. All three of these groups had questions about the danger from heavy textbooks (Parker-Pope, 2009).

The publishers replied honestly to the questions. They stated that they recently had been expanding the number of pages in textbooks in order to accommodate more instructional features. They lamented that these additional pages, which had been requested by teachers and endorsed by many parents, had increased the weight of the books.

The publishers also had been under pressure to make their books more durable. They had accomplished this through heavier paper, sturdier bindings, and thicker covers. They again acknowledged that these features, which had been requested by school administrators and endorsed by many parents, had increased the weight of the books.

The publishers had one final rejoinder for critics. They pointed out that their newer textbooks were not only heavier than earlier ones but also costlier to produce, store, and ship. As a result, they were earning a smaller profit.

Some parents were still angry with the publishers. Those who resided in California were especially irate. They asked their state legislators to specify maximum weights for textbooks.

California legislators enacted the law that the parents had requested. Within it, they specified the total weight of the textbooks that were used for core subjects. They limited this weight to three pounds for kindergarten through fourth-grade textbooks. They increased the weight by one pound for middle school textbooks and by two pounds for high school textbooks (California Department of Education, 2016).

The publishers were upset by the "heavy book" campaign. They assumed that it was damaging them. They conferred with their marketers about how to handle it.

The marketers told their clients to relax. They acknowledged that the campaign had tried to demonstrate that publishers had low regard for children. However, it inadvertently had demonstrated that the publishers were paying attention to suggestions from school administrators, teachers, and many parents. As a result, it actually had enhanced the publishers' image.

POSING QUESTIONS ABOUT PROMOTIONAL CAMPAIGNS

Marketers historically had encouraged politicians to avoid negative publicity. They had given the same advice to textbook publishers. However, they later realized that both groups could benefit from this publicity.

Activity 4.1

Marketers historically had charged their political clients to create positive publicity for them. They guaranteed them that they would benefit from it. How did groups respond?

Table 4.1 identifies two groups: political candidates and voters.

Complete the table by indicating the ways in which the groups responded to the marketers. You can use symbols.

Use the symbol – if the groups expressed low confidence in them. Use the symbol ± for moderate confidence and the symbol + for high confidence. As a final step, explain the basis for the symbols that you selected.

You can rely on the information in this chapter, additional information, or the information cited in the references. If you are reading this chapter with colleagues, you can confer with them.

Table 4.1. Marketers Assure Political Clients That They Will Benefit from Positive Publicity

Groups	Response*	Explanation
Candidates		
Voters		

* – Low
  ± Moderate
  + High

Activity 4.2

The marketers were struck by the amount of negative publicity surrounding the 2016 presidential election. They noted that it paradoxically was benefiting the candidates at whom it was directed. How did the groups respond?

Table 4.2 identifies two groups: political candidates and voters.

Complete the table by indicating the ways in which the groups responded to the marketers. You can use symbols.

Use the symbol – if the groups expressed low confidence in them. Use the symbol ± for moderate confidence and the symbol + for high confidence. As a final step, explain the basis for the symbols that you selected.

Table 4.2. Marketers Notice That Some Clients Benefit from Negative Publicity

Groups	Response*	Explanation
Candidates		
Voters		

* − Low
± Moderate
\+ High

Activity 4.3

Marketers historically had charged publishers to create positive publicity for textbooks. They guaranteed them that they would benefit from it. How did groups respond?

Table 4.3 identifies two groups: textbook publishers and parents with children in the public schools.

Complete the table by indicating the ways in which the groups responded to the marketers. You can use symbols.

Use the symbol − if the groups expressed low confidence in them. Use the symbol ± for moderate confidence and the symbol + for high confidence. As a final step, explain the basis for the symbols that you selected.

Table 4.3. Marketers Assure Textbook Publishers That They Will Benefit from Positive Publicity

Groups	Response*	Explanation
Publishers		
Parents		

* − Low
± Moderate
\+ High

Activity 4.4

The marketers were struck by the amount of negative publicity surrounding the campaign to restrict textbook weights. They noted that, paradoxically, it was benefiting the publishers at whom it was directed. How did groups respond?

Table 4.4 identifies two groups: textbook publishers and parents with children in the public schools.

Complete the table by indicating the ways in which the groups responded to the marketers. You can use symbols.

Use the symbol – if the groups expressed low confidence in them. Use the symbol ± for moderate confidence and the symbol + for high confidence. As a final step, explain the basis for the symbols that you selected.

Table 4.4. Marketers Notice That Some Publishers Benefit from Negative Publicity

Groups	Response*	Explanation
Publishers		
Parents		

* – Low
± Moderate
+ High

SUMMARY

Marketers historically had directed politicians to suppress negative publicity. They had given the same advice to textbook publishers. However, they later realized that textbook publishers actually could benefit from it.

Chapter Five

Do New Yorkers Have the Right Idea about Textbooks?

[Traditional commercial textbooks are] of questionable quality. —EngageNY Report, quoted by Pondiscio, 2015

[New York will replace traditional commercial textbooks with a free] online library of academic materials. —Educational journalist Sean Cavanagh, 2015

[New York's online library is] an important alternative to traditional textbooks. —Thomas B. Fordham Institute Fellows Kathleen Porter-Magee and Victoria McDougald, 2015

[When you use free online materials, you] get what you paid for. —Middle school teacher Heather Walpert-Gawron, quoted by Brody, 2017

Federal nominees had to respond to tough questions. State education commissioners faced the same challenge. They both resorted to robotic answers.

A FEDERAL NOMINEE USES ROBOTIC ANSWERS

Political candidates calculated the steps that they would have to take to become president. They quickly discovered that they needed to gather money and endorsements.

Jeb Bush hoped to become president in 2016. He was strategically in a good position. He had more cash than his competitors. He also had more endorsements than them.

Donald Trump was one of Bush's competitors. He readily acknowledged that he had less cash and fewer endorsements than Bush. However, he insisted that he still was a stronger candidate than Bush.

Trump characterized Bush as a stereotypical Washington insider. He stated that he would be a better choice than Bush precisely because he was a non-stereotypical candidate. He promised that, should he win, he would surround himself with like-minded cabinet members.

Trump won the election. When he had to nominate individuals for his cabinet, he made sure to choose some who were atypical. For example, he nominated Betsy DeVos, a citizen activist, to serve as his secretary of education (Zernike, 2016 November 23).

Enthusiasts

Although DeVos had been nominated for a cabinet position, she could not be immediately appointed. She first had to survive a Senate confirmation hearing.

Several confidantes helped DeVos get ready for that hearing. They warned her that she would face challenging questions during a nationally televised forum.

The confidantes gave DeVos a strategy for responding to her first difficult question: she should say that she would defer to states, local school districts, and parents. They encouraged her to use this strategy when responding to subsequent questions.

During the actual confirmation hearing, DeVos was asked whether she would increase federal funding to charter schools. She responded that she would allow states, local school districts, and parents to make this decision.

DeVos was asked whether she would use federal funds to pay for vouchers at private schools. She responded that she would allow states, local school districts, and parents to make this decision.

DeVos was asked about the federal government's role in tests, school discipline, teacher evaluation, guns on campuses, for-profit schools, and programs for children with disabilities. In every instance, she responded that she would turn to states, local school districts, and parents for advice.

Skeptics

Some senators were furious with the manner in which DeVos responded to their questions. They demanded that she withdraw from consideration.

DeVos would not step aside. She insisted that she had the experience and temperament to serve as secretary of education. She was relieved when the president reaffirmed his confidence in her ("Trump on Twitter," 2017).

DeVos's critics wished to block her appointment. However, they realized that they did not have enough votes. They therefore turned to journalists and asked them to stir up the public.

The journalists at the *New York Times* were eager to help. They depicted DeVos as a mindless ideologue who had "robotically" responded to the questions at her hearing. They concluded that she had provided a chilling lesson about the "value of ignorance" (*New York Times* Editorial Board, 2016a; 2017a, 2017b).

Not all journalists attacked DeVos. Some of them actually commended her. They noted that she had been dealing with hostile senators during her confirmation hearing. They admired the way in which she had deflected their disingenuous questions (Goldstein, 2017; *Wall Street Journal* Editorial Board, 2017d, 2017e).

The pro-DeVos journalists and the anti-DeVos journalists argued back and forth. However, they wondered how their readers were reacting to this sparring. They were especially curious about parents.

Parents historically had not shown much interest in the secretary of education. As evidence, few of them could identify a single individual who had served in that position (Annenberg Public Policy Center, 2014).

In spite of a tradition of apathy, some parents did publicize their displeasure with DeVos. One group blocked her from visiting a school; another encouraged their children to stage a school walkout (Bellafante, 2017; Firozi, 2017; Toure, 2017).

A STATE COMMISSIONER USES ROBOTIC ANSWERS

New York is a heavily populated state. It has millions of students, thousands of schools, and hundreds of local school boards.

The local school boards in New York had important responsibilities. For example, they had to designate textbooks.

Although the members of the district school boards had the authority to designate textbooks, they rarely acted on their own. They instead consulted with their superintendents.

When the superintendents had to give advice about textbooks, they also were collaborative. They consulted their principals, curriculum directors, instructional specialists, departmental chairs, teachers, and parents. They also made sure to consult with the staff at the New York State Education Department (NYSDE).

The staff at the NYSDE had the final authority over textbooks. They could disqualify any textbook that was not aligned with the state's curricula (New York State Education Department, 2017).

The superintendents were aware of the NYSDE's textbook authority. They therefore contacted its staff members before purchasing any instructional materials. They wanted to make sure they approved.

If the superintendents obtained approval for textbooks, they went ahead and purchased them. If they did not obtain it, they could select other books. Alternatively, they could appeal the staff's decision. They would make this appeal to the state commissioner of education.

Enthusiasts

The commissioner of education led the NYSDE. The New York superintendents did not underestimate this person.

The superintendents realized that the commissioner had a major impact on them, their staffs, their schools, and their students. For this reason, they were nervous whenever a new commissioner was appointed.

The superintendents were on edge in 2011, after Commissioner David Steiner announced his resignation. They wondered who would follow him.

John King was Steiner's replacement. He made the superintendents anxious when he announced that he would be making changes. He stated that some of these changes had been foreshadowed in a recent grant proposal.

Commissioner Steiner had submitted the grant proposal to which King had referred. In fact, Steiner was still commissioner when that proposal was funded. However, he had left the implementation to his successor.

King announced that the grant required him to take several important steps. One of the most important was the creation of an online library of classroom materials. He referred to this library as EngageNY.

New York's superintendents were anxious about the online materials. They immediately had a practical question. Would they have to give up their textbooks and use the online materials instead?

King recognized that the superintendents were anxious. He therefore assured them that they still would be able to use traditional textbooks.

Skeptics

The superintendents later went back to the commissioner. They explained that they were still anxious because his staffers had been directing them to retire traditional textbooks and substitute the online materials from EngageNY. They asked whether they had to follow the staffers' directives.

King gave the superintendents the answer that he had given earlier. He stated that they were under no pressure to use online materials. He told them that they could still use traditional textbooks if they preferred.

King served as commissioner for more than three years. During that time, he had to respond to numerous questions about the online materials at EngageNY.

Although the questions came from superintendents, they also came from parents (Douglas-Gabriel & Layton, 2016; Korn, 2016a; Taylor, 2014).

The parents made it clear that they were not impressed by the online materials. They posed challenging questions about the content in them, the pedagogy on which they were based, and even the copyediting of the passages within them ("Is NYSED," 2014).

King responded robotically. He stated that he was not pressuring the parents to use materials from EngageNY in their children's schools. He insisted that they still could use traditional textbooks.

DEALING WITH ROBOTIC ANSWERS

Federal nominees had to respond to challenging questions. State education commissioners also had to respond to them. They both resorted to robotic responses.

Activity 5.1

Nominees for federal cabinet positions faced challenging questions. They historically had provided straightforward answers. How did groups respond?

Table 5.1 identifies two groups: senators and parents.

Complete the table by indicating the ways in which the groups responded to the nominees. You can use symbols.

Use the symbol – if the groups expressed low confidence in them. Use the symbol ± for moderate confidence and the symbol + for high confidence. As a final step, explain the basis for the symbols that you selected.

You can rely on the information in this chapter, additional information, or the information cited in the references. If you are reading this chapter with colleagues, you can confer with them.

Table 5.1. Cabinet Nominees Provide Straightforward Answers

Groups	Response*	Explanation
Senators		
Parents		

* – Low
± Moderate
+ High

Activity 5.2

When Betsy DeVos was nominated for secretary of education, she faced challenging questions. She resorted to robotic answers. How did the groups respond?

Table 5.2 identifies two groups: senators and parents.

Complete the table by indicating the ways in which the groups responded to this nominee. You can use symbols.

Use the symbol – if the groups expressed low confidence in her. Use the symbol ± for moderate confidence and the symbol + for high confidence. As a final step, explain the basis for the symbols that you selected.

Table 5.2. A Nominee Provides Robotic Answers

Groups	Response*	Explanation
Senators		
Parents		

* – Low
± Moderate
+ High

Activity 5.3

New York's commissioners of education faced challenging questions about textbooks. They historically had provided straightforward answers. How did groups respond?

Table 5.3 identifies two groups: superintendents and parents.

Complete the table by indicating the ways in which the groups responded to the commissioners. You can use symbols.

Use the symbol – if the groups expressed low confidence in them. Use the symbol ± for moderate confidence and the symbol + for high confidence. As a final step, explain the basis for the symbols that you selected.

Table 5.3. Commissioners of Education Provide Straightforward Answers

Groups	Response*	Explanation
Superintends		
Parents		

* – Low
± Moderate
+ High

Activity 5.4

Commissioner of Education King faced challenging questions about textbooks. He resorted to robotic answers. How did the groups respond?

Table 5.4 identifies two groups: superintendents and parents.

Complete the table by indicating the ways in which the groups responded to this commissioner. You can use symbols.

Use the symbol – if the groups expressed low confidence in him. Use the symbol ± for moderate confidence and the symbol + for high confidence. As a final step, explain the basis for the symbols that you selected.

Table 5.4. A Commissioner Provides Robotic Answers

Groups	Response*	Explanation
Superintends		
Parents		

* – Low
± Moderate
+ High

SUMMARY

Federal nominees had to respond to difficult questions. State commissioners of education faced the same challenge. They resorted to robotic answers.

Chapter Six

Do Publishers Have the Right Idea about Textbooks?

[The publishers at our firm have] the highest industry standards for fairness and quality. —Unidentified Pearson spokesperson, quoted by Brody, 2016

Our products . . . are used by millions of teachers. —Pearson PLC, 2017

[The publishers at Pearson control] the tests students take [and] the textbooks they read. —Journalist Laura Clawson, 2015

[Any] changes . . . in a textbook [become] profitable. —Former Pearson executive Kim Koerber, quoted by Berry, 2016

Publishers of academic journals were under pressure to control prices. Publishers of textbooks were under similar pressure. They came up with innovative ways to comply.

CONTROLLING JOURNAL PRICES

Publishers needed sound business plans. They had to be sure that they would address the products that they created, the amount of capital they invested, the audience to which they sold their products, and the prices that they charged.

The publishers had to decide whether to provide general materials to a wide audience or specialized materials to a smaller one. They realized that the first approach required a large investment, while the second one required a much smaller one.

The publishers then had to make another important decision: they had to designate how to set prices. They had good reasons to set them high, because they needed to pay for author royalties, printing, storage, distribution, and advertising. Nonetheless, they still had to be careful, as they did not want to set the price so high that their products became noncompetitive on the market.

The large publishers devised a straightforward business plan. They would sell low-priced products to the widest possible audience. They believed that they could cover costs and still make a profit because sales volume would be high.

Small publishers conceded that they could not compete by marketing the same products as the larger firms. They, therefore, investigated products in which the large firms were not interested. Some of them investigated academic journals.

Two groups of customers bought academic journals. Professors purchased them so that they could gather information about scholarly fields of study. University librarians purchased them so that they could make that information available on their campuses.

The small publishers calculated the amount of money they could make from academic journals. Some believed that it was too little for them to get involved. However, others remained optimistic.

The publishers who were interested in academic journals realized that these materials had extremely modest production costs. They noted that professors wrote for them without any compensation.

The publishers who became involved with academic journals had to rely on subscribers for all of their income. When they were not collecting enough, they had to raise their subscription rates (Masnick, 2011).

Enthusiasts

After they had hiked prices, publishers kept an eye on their subscribers. They wanted to find out how they were reacting.

The professors were annoyed. The librarians shared these sentiments. They looked for ways to show the publishers how they felt.

The professors showed their displeasure by canceling their subscriptions. Although the librarians wished to follow their example, they could not. They were obligated to provide campus-wide access to the journals.

The publishers noted that they had kept their library customers even after the price hikes. They therefore decided to raise their prices even higher: they announced that they would bill librarians at a substantially higher rate than other subscribers. They explained that differential pricing made sense because the librarians paid for a single copy of a journal but then shared it with numerous patrons (Bosch & Henderson, 2015; Swoger, 2012).

Skeptics

The university librarians were extremely upset about the higher prices of academic journals. They complained to the publishers.

The publishers listened to the distraught librarians. They assured them that they understood their concerns. They pledged that they would find a strategy to control prices.

After the publishers had made that pledge, they were in a bind. They would need more income to remain in business. However, they had only one option left: They would have to go to professors for the money.

The publishers came up with a clever strategy. They directed it at those professors who wrote for their journals. They told the professors that they would have to pay special compositing fees. The publishers explained that they had to levy these new fees in order to keep their journal prices down. They urged the professors to understand their perilous financial situation, support their actions, and pay the fees.

Professors asked their universities to reimburse them for the compositing fees. When they were reimbursed, they paid the publishers and did not complain. Even many of the professors who were not reimbursed still paid the publishers. Although they complained, they felt that they had to come up with the money in order to meet the expectations of their jobs (Carey, 2016; Yudkevich, 2012).

Some professors were extremely agitated about the compositing fees. After forming an alliance with university librarians, they publicly berated the publishers for their predatory practices (Beall, 2012; Straumsheim, 2017).

CONTROLLING TEXTBOOK PRICES

The early publishers anticipated that schools would be lucrative markets. They were excited by opportunities to supply them with printed classroom materials. However, they first had to hire personnel to write, illustrate, edit, and market these specialized materials (Giordano, 2004).

At the beginning of the twentieth century, dozens of firms were creating textbooks and generating profits from them. However, few of them made enough money to sustain their ventures. By the end of the century, a relatively small group remained in business. The Pearson Corporation was the largest member of the group (Giordano, 2004).

The Pearson Corporation dominated the textbook market because of its impressive personnel resources. It had thousands of employees with specialized skills. It also had scores of executives with strategic acumen (Pearson PLC, 2015, 2017).

The Pearson Corporation also had impressive monetary resources. It spent a good portion of this money creating premium textbooks. It spent another portion on government lobbying.

The Pearson executives regularly reviewed the amount that they were spending. They eventually concluded that it was too high. They worried that it would cause profits to deteriorate.

The Pearson executives needed a way to compensate for their spending. They came up with a straightforward strategy: They would raise prices. They were not the first publisher to take this action. Leaders in their industry had been increasing textbook prices for some time. In fact, they had increased them by 800 percent during the final decades of the twentieth century (Band, 2013; Giordano, 2003).

After the Pearson executives began increasing prices, they noted that profits increased along with them. Although they were pleased, they were nervous about alienating their customers. They worried particularly about the school administrators who purchased their textbooks (Trex, 2011).

Enthusiasts

The Pearson executives discovered that school administrators were concerned about climbing textbook prices. They assured them that they understood their concerns. They pledged to find a strategy to control prices.

The Pearson executives eventually unveiled their strategy: they would be discounting some textbook prices. However, they added a caveat: they would be discounting prices only on those textbooks that were purchased in bundles. They explained that the bundles could include additional types of textbooks and also student workbooks, online learning materials, tests, or test-preparation materials (Reingold, 2015).

The executives assured school administrators that bundling allowed them to purchase products at lower prices. They hoped that school administrators would be enthusiastic about it.

The executives hoped that corporate investors also would be enthusiastic about bundling. They explained that the bundling of modestly profitable products with highly profitable ones would cause a spike in the firm's net revenue (Koch, 2006; Zekaria, 2015).

Skeptics

Some school administrators were impressed by the discounts associated with bundling. However, others were skeptical. The skeptics noted that their textbook bills were higher than ever. They lamented that they had to divert funds from other critical areas in order to pay those bills (Giordano, 2014; Rapp, 2008).

The school administrators wanted the Pearson executives to make steeper price cuts. When they could not get a commitment from the school administrators, the Pearson executives, resolved to exert pressure on them. However, they realized that they would need help.

The school administrators went to journalists. They asked them to publicize the problems that Pearson had created through aggressive price hikes.

The journalists listened to the school administrators. They were eager to investigate their allegations. However, they still needed to hear the executives' side in this dispute.

The Pearson executives conceded that they had been raising the prices of their textbooks. However, they added that they simultaneously had been making revisions to those textbooks. They stated that they had to raise the prices to cover the expenses of the revisions.

Some teachers challenged the executives' claims. They contended that the firm's latest textbooks had few substantive changes from earlier editions (Barrow, 2016).

The journalists wondered whether the Pearson executives had an ulterior motive for increasing prices. They suspected that they were trying to raise money to cover their expanding political lobbying activities (Clawson, 2015; Simon, 2016; Zekaria, 2016).

The journalists noted that the Pearson executives, who sold tests as well as textbooks, had been urging government officials to purchase both of these products from their firm. The journalists assumed that the money from the textbook hikes was being used to fund political contributions to these officials (Figueroa, 2013; Kamenetz, 2106; Strauss, 2015).

POSING QUESTIONS ABOUT TEXTBOOK PRICING

When publishers were criticized for the high prices of academic journals, they pledged to find a strategy to control them. When they were criticized for the high prices of textbooks, they repeated this pledge. They searched for strategies to appease critics without affecting their income.

Activity 6.1

Publishers wished to increase the revenue from academic journals. They therefore raised the prices. How did groups respond?

Table 6.1 identifies two groups: university librarians and professors.

Complete the table by indicating the ways in which these groups responded to the publishers. You can use symbols.

Use the symbol – if the groups expressed low confidence in them. Use the symbol ± for moderate confidence and the symbol + for high confidence. As a final step, explain the basis for the symbols that you selected.

You can rely on the information in this chapter, additional information, or the information cited in the references. If you are reading this chapter with colleagues, you can confer with them.

Table 6.1. Publishers Hike Journal Prices

Groups	Response*	Explanation
Librarians		
Professors		

* – Low
± Moderate
+ High

Activity 6.2

Publishers were criticized for excessively high journal prices. They pledged to control them through author-paid fees. How did the groups respond?

Table 6.2 identifies two groups: university librarians and professors.

Complete the table by indicating the ways in which these groups responded to the publishers. You can use symbols.

Use the symbol – if the groups expressed low confidence in them. Use the symbol ± for moderate confidence and the symbol + for high confidence. As a final step, explain the basis for the symbols that you selected.

Table 6.2. Publishers Control Journal Prices with Author-Paid Fees

Groups	Response*	Explanation
Librarians		
Professors		

* – Low
± Moderate
+ High

Activity 6.3

Publishers wished to increase the revenue from textbooks. They therefore raised prices. How did groups respond?

Table 6.3 identifies two groups: investors and educators.

Complete the table by indicating the ways in which these groups responded to the publishers. You can use symbols.

Use the symbol – if the groups expressed low confidence in them. Use the symbol ± for moderate confidence and the symbol + for high confidence. As a final step, explain the basis for the symbols that you selected.

Table 6.3. Publishers Hike Textbook Prices

Groups	Response*	Explanation
Investors		
Educators		

* – Low
± Moderate
+ High

Activity 6.4

Publishers were criticized for excessively high textbook prices. They pledged to control them through bundled purchasing discounts. How did the groups respond?

Table 6.4 identifies two groups: investors and educators.

Complete the table by indicating the ways in which these groups responded to the publishers. You can use symbols.

Use the symbol – if the groups expressed low confidence in them. Use the symbol ± for moderate confidence and the symbol + for high confidence. As a final step, explain the basis for the symbols that you selected.

Table 6.4. Publishers Control Textbook Prices with Bundled Purchasing Discounts

Groups	Response*	Explanation
Investors		
Educators		

* – Low
± Moderate
+ High

SUMMARY

Publishers were criticized for the high prices of academic journals and textbooks. They pledged to reduce the journal prices through author-paid fees. They pledged to reduce the textbook prices through discounts on bundled purchases. They were eager to see how critics would react.

Chapter Seven

Do Parents Have the Right Idea about Textbooks?

[Florida's legislators are] eliminating the lay [textbook] committees. —Journalist Bill Maxwell, 2011

Encourage Governor Scott to protect lay participation [on the textbook committees]. —Florida Freedom Council, 2011

[Lay textbook committees are needed to block school materials that are] teaching . . . that the government is our nanny. —Florida Citizens' Alliance managing director Keith Flaugh, quoted by Spencer, 2017

Florida [has passed a new] law that encourages parents . . . to review [textbooks once again]. —Florida Citizens' Alliance, 2017

University students had concerns about the information that professors presented to them. Parents had concerns about the information that public school textbooks presented to their children. Both groups demanded changes.

EMPOWERING UNIVERSITY STUDENTS

Professors regularly presented students with provocative information. They told them that this critically important information had to be presented in an unsettling fashion.

The students disagreed. They contended that the professors were being unnecessarily hurtful. They asked them to exhibit greater civility. They were disappointed when the professors refused.

The students were not ready to give up. They appealed to the presidents of their universities. They gave them examples of the offensive language that professors had used when referring to race, ethnicity, religion, economic status, gender, disabilities, and sexual orientation. They also gave examples of the insensitive manner in which they had discussed topics such as rape, child abuse, and abortion (Downes, 2016).

The students had a solution for the problems they had highlighted. They suggested that their professors restrict the language that they used and the topics that they covered. They wanted those who would not comply to be punished.

The presidents listened respectfully to the students. However, they noted the professors might not even be aware of terms and topics that the students judged to be troublesome.

The students had a rejoinder. They suggested that the professors issue warnings before presenting any information that might "trigger" negative reactions. They explained that these warnings would give students a chance to decide whether they should vacate the classrooms (Wright, 2015).

University presidents assured their students that they did not want them to feel threatened or marginalized. They promised to make classroom "trigger warnings" mandatory.

Enthusiasts

The students commended the presidents who backed trigger warnings. However, they were accused by the faculty of restricting academic freedom. Needless to say, they disagreed.

The students explained that academic freedom did not give professors the right to be discourteous and offensive. They adjured them to embrace trigger warnings. They were disheartened by those who still refused (West, 2015).

The students resolved to escalate their fight. However, they knew that their professors would be formidable adversaries. They needed allies if they were going to win these confrontations. They therefore contacted journalists. They were excited when many of them took their side in the dispute (Gay, 2015; Moynihan, 2017; Simon, 2016).

The students were pleased with the journalists who endorsed trigger warnings. They hoped that they also would endorse punishments for professors who ignored them (Wright, 2015).

Skeptics

Robert Zimmer was the president of the University of Chicago. Like leaders on other campuses, he listened to disgruntled students. He paid special attention when they requested trigger warnings.

Zimmer wanted to be responsive to his students. However, he also wished to be responsive to his donors. He learned that some of his university's most influential donors saw little value in trigger warnings.

Zimmer had to choose whether to side with the students or the donors. After he had made up his mind, he confided to the donors that he shared their skepticism about trigger warnings. He vowed that he would never implement them. He directed one of his deans to communicate this decision to the students.

The president's message was sent only to those students who were about to enter the university. Nonetheless, it fell into the hands of the students who already had been admitted, who had been attending lectures, who had been upset by them, and who had requested trigger warnings.

The students who advocated trigger warnings felt that Zimmer had betrayed them. They accused him of posturing for donors at their expense (Downes, 2016; Gay, 2015; Pérez-Peña, Smith, & Saul, 2016).

EMPOWERING PARENTS

Parents were interested in their children's textbooks. They therefore examined them carefully. They wished to make sure that the textbooks had appropriate language and accurate information.

When the parents detected offensive textbooks, they protested to teachers and principals. Some of them went further and protested to their superintendents.

All of these educators listened respectfully to the parents. Some even indicated that they shared their concerns. However, they explained that they had purchased the textbooks and did not have the money to replace them. They asked the parents to be understanding.

The parents were irate. Those who resided in Florida were especially irate. They told the educators that they wanted opportunities to review potential textbooks before they were purchased.

The educators tried to calm the parents. They explained that textbooks were screened by special state committees. They urged the parents to investigate the rules governing these committees.

The parents did study the committee rules. They discovered that they limited membership to educators, personnel from the Florida State Department of Education (FLDOE), and some specially appointed members (Florida Department of Education, 2017).

The parents were upset about the membership rules for the textbook committees. They demanded that they be changed so that they could be appointed to the committees.

The legislators were reluctant to accommodate the parents. They feared that they would create a commotion on textbook committees. However, they realized that they currently were creating a commotion because they were excluded from them. The legislators offered them a compromise: they would appoint a single parental representative to each textbook committee.

The parents ardently wanted to review textbooks. They therefore accepted this offer. They were especially eager to review those for science classes. They wanted to see whether the textbooks acknowledged the role of a divine being when they were explaining the origin of human life (Allen, 2017).

The parents also were eager to review prospective history textbooks. They wanted to find out how they depicted America's economy and system of government. They approved of books that employed a flattering tone; they disapproved of those that did not (Florida Citizens' Alliance, 2017; Postal, 2017).

Enthusiasts

Florida's legislators had listened to parents. They also had followed their advice: They had allowed them to sit on textbook committees. They assumed that they were grateful.

The parents were grateful. They sat on committees, voted on textbooks, and became activists when they disagreed with the votes of the other committee members. They frequently created a ruckus.

The legislators were rattled by the activist parents. They noted that they were attracting enormous media attention.

The textbook publishers also were rattled. They had followed an arduous and expensive process to create textbooks. They were distraught when disgruntled parents demanded that these books be scuttled.

The publishers urged the legislators to revise the textbook selection process. They gave them a single suggestion: exclude parents.

The legislators were in a bind. They depended on the publishers for campaign contributions; they depended on the parents for votes. They wished to appease both groups.

The legislators eventually came up with a plan. However, it required them to change their regulations again.

The legislators decided that parents would no longer review textbooks. Instead, two experts would review them. These experts would ask the same question about each book: Was it aligned with Florida's learning standards? If the experts came to the same conclusion, they would be finished with their task. If they did not agree, they would defer to a third expert, who would break their tie (Brayton, 2011).

The legislators informed the publishers of their new parent-free approach to regulating textbooks. They were confident that the publishers would approve.

Skeptics

Many parents were distraught about the new textbook regulations. Those who served on textbook committees were especially distraught. They accused their legislators of rewarding publishers at the expense of children.

The parents were ready to escalate their confrontation with the legislators. However, they needed assistance. They asked journalists to broadcast their concerns to readers, listeners, and viewers. They hoped that they would underscore the role that the publishers had played in the new textbook approval process (Maxwell, 2011).

Some of the legislators had campaigned on a pledge to combat special interests in public education. They were unnerved when they were accused of abandoning their pledge (Gordon, 2014; Swier, 2014).

The legislators repeatedly tried to explain their rationale for eliminating textbook committees. They contended that they only had wished to reduce the state's bureaucracy and save its money.

The parents were not swayed by the legislators. They were sure that they were being disingenuous. They threatened to show their displeasure during the next election (Florida Freedom Council, 2011).

The legislators had underestimated the parents. They wished to end their confrontation with them. They ideally wished to regain their confidence.

Although they did wish to regain the confidence of parents, the legislators still wished to retain that of publishers. They concluded that they would have to find an ingenious way to make both groups happy.

The legislators decided to amend the textbook law again. In the newest version of it, they stipulated that the FLDOE would continue to arrange expert reviews. However, they added that local school districts could arrange parental reviews.

The legislators insisted that parental textbook reviews had been reinstated. They noted that these reviews would be posted on a special FLDOE website. They predicted that they then would be read by staff members at the FLDOE as well as those at the textbook firms ("Florida Legislature Passes," 2014).

While they were speaking publicly to parents, the legislators were speaking privately to publishers. They told the publishers that the FLDOE would be allowing—but not requiring—local districts to gather parental textbook reviews.

Publishers and parents carefully examined the new regulations. The publishers, who concluded that the FLDOE would be making the final decisions about textbooks, felt pleased. However, the parents, who reached

60   *Chapter Seven*

the identical conclusion, felt bamboozled ("Amend Florida SB 864," 2017; Clark, 2017: Goodman, 2017; Kaplan, 2017; Ross, 2017)

DEALING WITH DISINGENUOUS ANSWERS

College students posed questions about unsettling lectures. Parents posed them about unsettling pubic school textbooks. Disappointed by the answers that they received, both groups resolved to get more involved.

Activity 7.1

University presidents realized that students were upset by professors' lectures. They therefore required the professors to use trigger warnings. How did groups respond?

Table 7.1 identifies two groups: students and donors.

Complete the table by indicating the ways in which the groups responded to the presidents. You can use symbols.

Use the symbol – if the groups expressed low confidence in them. Use the symbol ± for moderate confidence and the symbol + for high confidence. As a final step, explain the basis for the symbols that you selected.

You can rely on the information in this chapter, additional information, or the information cited in the references. If you are reading this chapter with colleagues, you can confer with them.

Table 7.1. University Presidents Implement Trigger Warnings

Groups	Response*	Explanation
Students		
Donors		

* – Low
  ± Moderate
  + High

Activity 7.2

President Zimmer believed that the University of Chicago's students would abuse trigger warnings. He announced that his professors would not have to use them. How did the groups respond?

Do Parents Have the Right Idea about Textbooks? 61

Table 7.2 identifies two groups at this university: students and donors.

Complete the table by indicating the ways in which the groups responded to the president. You can use symbols.

Use the symbol – if the groups expressed low confidence in him. Use the symbol ± for moderate confidence and the symbol + for high confidence. As a final step, explain the basis for the symbols that you selected.

Table 7.2. A University President Refuses to Implement Trigger Warnings

Groups	Response*	Explanation
Students		
Donors		

* – Low
± Moderate
+ High

Activity 7.3

Florida's legislators realized that parents were upset by the textbooks that the state screening committees had approved. They therefore appointed a parental representative to every committee. How did groups respond?

Table 7.3 identifies two groups: parents and textbook publishers.

Complete the table by indicating the ways in which the groups responded to the legislators. You can use symbols.

Use the symbol – if the groups expressed low confidence in them. Use the symbol ± for moderate confidence and the symbol + for high confidence. As a final step, explain the basis for the symbols that you selected.

Table 7.3. Florida's Legislators Appoint Parents to State Textbook Committees

Groups	Response*	Explanation
Parents		
Publishers		

* – Low
± Moderate
+ High

Activity 7.4

Florida's legislators believed that the parental representatives were abusing their authority on textbook screening committees. They announced that they would disband the committees. How did the groups respond?

Table 7.4 identifies two groups: parents and textbook publishers.

Complete the table by indicating the ways in which the groups responded to the legislators. You can use symbols.

Use the symbol – if the groups expressed low confidence in them. Use the symbol ± for moderate confidence and the symbol + for high confidence. As a final step, explain the basis for the symbols that you selected.

Table 7.4. **Florida's Legislators Disband State Textbook Committees**

Groups	Response*	Explanation
Parents		
Publishers		

* – Low
 ± Moderate
 + High

SUMMARY

College students were unsettled by the lectures on their campuses. Parents were unsettled by the textbooks in the public schools. Although both groups demanded changes, they were disappointed by the responses to their demands.

Chapter Eight

Do Floridians Have the Right Idea about Textbooks?

[Jeb Bush] attempted to paint [himself] as a governor who was ahead of his time when it came to technology. —Journalist Ashley Killough, 2015

The e-books [that Jeb Bush has endorsed] are rubbish. —Anonymous parent, responding to an editorial by Jeb Bush, 2013

[Jeb Bush] "dumbed down" Florida schools. —Former Florida state senator Dan Gelber, 2015

[Jeb] Bush's . . . educational philosophy has been soundly rejected by parents. —Tea Party Network chairwoman Catherine Baer, quoted by Larrabee, 2017c

Florida's legislators were under pressure to change some of their laws. They focused on the sales laws affecting liquor and the purchasing laws affecting textbooks.

RESTRICTING LIQUOR

Florida's legislators regulated sales of over-the-counter alcohol. They historically had relied on a two-pronged distribution system. They allowed supermarkets, drugstores, and gas stations to sell beer and wine. They permitted only specially designated stores to sell distilled spirits.

Floridians did not understand why their legislators handled beer and wine differently than distilled spirits. They asked them for an explanation.

The legislators replied that they were concerned about children stealing alcohol. They did not worry about them taking beer or wine, which came in containers that were too large to pilfer. However, they believed that they could easily steal "hard" liquor because of the smaller containers in which it was packaged. For these reasons, they allowed sales of beer and wine in supermarkets, drugstores, and gas stations but restricted sales of liquor to specialty stores (Turner, 2017).

The legislators used a metaphor to describe their regulations. They proclaimed that they had created a "wall" that kept hard liquor away from children.

Enthusiasts

Some citizens commended their legislators. They believed that they were keeping youngsters safe (Call, 2017).

The owners of liquor stores was eager to commend the legislators. They realized that they had given them a monopoly on liquor sales. They hired lobbyists to communicate their approval (Mulrooney, 2017).

The lobbyists paid the legislators compliments; they also paid them money. They made it clear that both would continue only if they kept the wall in place (Turner, 2017).

Skeptics

The retailers who owned supermarkets, drugstores, and gas stations had listened attentively when their state legislators had stated that they were interested in protecting children. However, they were unconvinced. They were sure that they were more interested in securing campaign donations ("Tear Down," 2017).

The disgruntled retailers wished to change the current liquor law. They decided to use the same strategy that the liquor store owners were using to keep the law in place: They would offer campaign donations. However, they would give them only to legislators who voted to make a change. They became excited when some of the legislators agreed to cooperate with them.

The legislators who switched course realized that some of their constituents would be disappointed by them. They tried to explain their reasoning. They stated that they had good intentions for originally supporting the wall. However, they changed their minds after they learned of the hardships that the wall was creating for liquor-buying consumers (Arnold, 2016).

The two legislative factions could not agree. They feuded over the best way to regulate liquor sales for years.

The members of the anti-liquor wall faction became more confident during the 2017 legislative session. They believed that they finally had the votes that they needed to dismantle the wall (*Sun Sentinel* Editorial Board, 2017; *Tallahassee Democrat* Editorial Board, 2017).

The pro-wall legislators sensed that they were about to lose. They searched for a way to strengthen their position. They hoped that a catchy message would help. They eventually devised one: They stated that they needed the wall to prevent their opponents from selling whiskey and Wheaties on the same store shelves (Mulrooney, 2017).

RESTRICTING TEXTBOOKS

Jeb Bush had always set lofty political goals. During the early stages of his career, he aspired to become governor of Florida.

Bush had begun competing for governor at the beginning of the 1990s. Even though he did not win the office at this time, he did not sulk. He began making plans for another election.

On his second run for governor, Bush was successful. He then established a long-term political goal: He intended to become president of the United States.

Bush began cultivating supporters for a national campaign. He concentrated on three groups: businesspeople, journalists, and conservative-leaning members of the public. He needed the first group for campaign funds, the second for media coverage, and the third for votes.

Bush searched for a trendy political topic to lure supporters. He chose education. He explained that he intended to foster charter schools, subsidize tuition at private schools, make curricula more demanding, administer more tests, retain low-performing students, and dismiss low-performing teachers (Giordano, 2015).

Bush had expected his educational plans to create excitement. He was devastated when they did not. He called in consultants and asked them why his plans had failed.

The consultants readily diagnosed the problem. They told Bush that his educational plans were out-of-date. They noted that his brother, George W. Bush, had used the same plans for a gubernatorial campaign in Texas and then later for a presidential campaign.

The consultants counseled Bush to come up with fresh educational ideas. They recommended that he concentrate on technology. They suggested that he showcase a Florida school that relied heavily on technology, take credit for it, and then designate it as a model for other schools (Bush, 2013).

Bush was impressed by this advice. He began by identifying a model school—the Florida Virtual School (FLVS).

The FLVS had been created in 1997 to help parents who were homeschooling high-school-age children. It furnished online courses, computerized testing, and digital textbooks.

Bush wished to get persons excited about the FLVS. For example, he was concerned about businesspeople. He made a special appeal to those who were involved with technology. He convinced them that the FLVS would be a chance for them to advertise their products.

Bush also made a special appeal to journalists. He explained that FLVS was a topic that would enliven their educational reporting (Killough, 2015).

Bush was convinced that the FLVS would generate publicity for him. However, he realized that it had a major problem that he would have to solve.

The FLVS had received massive funding when it was established. It was expected to then sustain itself through state money that it would collect for serving students. Because it had served few students, it had collected hardly any funds.

Bush could have helped the FLVS through a special legislative allocation. However, he realized that the school was closely linked to homeschool parents. He worried that he would appear to be repaying these parents for the help that they had given him during the election (Berry, 2014).

Bush looked for a way to help the FLVS indirectly. He devised a clever plan: He would require that all of the state's high school students take an online course. He assumed that they would take it from the FLVS. He predicted that that school's enrollment and coffers would swell as a result (MacGillis, 2015).

Enthusiasts

Jeb Bush had portrayed himself as a person who could solve a state's educational problems. He made Florida's schools into a showcase for his talent. After he left the governor's office, he wished to represent himself as a person who could solve the nation's educational problems (Gabriel, 2011; Gelber, 2015).

Bush needed to generate media attention. He established a large public relations office: the Foundation for Educational Excellence. He directed it to highlight his educational accomplishments in Florida and his plan to replicate them nationwide (O'Connor, 2012; Layton, 2015).

Rick Scott followed Bush as Florida's governor. Since he had no experience with the public schools, he relied heavily on Bush. He was particularly interested in Bush's efforts to promote the FLVS.

Scott announced that he would continue to promote the FLVS. However, he quickly realized that it was not financially healthy. He therefore pleaded with state legislators for help. He wanted them to add FLVS-focused funds to the current educational budget.

The legislators did not wish to antagonize the governor. However, they also did not wish to allocate any more money to the state's current educational budget. They therefore offered a compromise. They would help the FLVS indirectly: They would divert a larger chunk of the education budget to that school.

Scott judged that the legislators' offer would enable the FLVS to continue operating. He therefore accepted it. However, he needed to sustain two more of Bush's digital scholastic programs: those involving eTests and eTextbooks. He went back to the legislator and requested additional money for these initiatives.

The legislators again refused the governor's request. However, they noted that they already were allocating funds for in-print tests and textbooks. They offered to shift some of the funds from in-print materials to digital materials ("Florida Legislature's," 2011; Larrabee, 2017a, 2017b; "Textbooks in All," 2011).

The legislators were relieved when Scott agreed to all of their proposals. However, they still were nervous about Jeb Bush. They realized that Bush, even though he was no longer governor, had enormous power in their state. They wished to get his approval.

Bush carefully reviewed the legislators' plan. After he was convinced that it would not harm his educational legacy, he gave his approval (Killough, 2015; Velderman, 2014).

The legislators were concerned about publishers as well as political leaders. They depended on the publishers for campaign contributions. They wondered how they were reacting to their funding shifts.

The publishers placed a high priority on digital products. They were aware that they made higher profits from them than they did from in-print products. They told the legislators that they enthusiastically would support any steps to expand sales of digital products (Giordano, 2003, 2015, 2016).

The legislators were concerned about the reaction of one more group—parents. They depended on them for votes. They wondered how they were responding to their actions.

Parents who were homeschooling their children had benefited from digital education. They believed that eTests and eTextbooks were important components of that initiative. They therefore supported the legislators.

Even many parents who were not homeschooling their children had benefited from digital education. Like the homeschooling parents, they had confidence in eTests and eTextbooks. They believed that the use of these resources was propelling Florida's schools into national prominence. They supported the legislators (Tomassini, 2012).

Skeptics

Parents in Florida listened to Jeb Bush while he was their governor. Some of them supported his attempts to push educational technology into schools; others did not. The skeptics questioned his motives. They suspected that he had conflicts of interest.

The skeptical parents endured Bush for eight years. They were hopeful that his successor, Rick Scott, would adopt a distinct approach to schools. They were dejected when he did not.

The disconsolate parents resolved to resist Scott. They noted that he was a political neophyte who only recently had become involved in state government. They anticipated that he would be less formidable than Bush.

Even though the parents were hopeful of a victory against their new governor, they realized that they would need allies. They therefore asked public school administrators and teachers to join them. They were excited when both groups accepted the invitation.

The parents and educators were a powerful coalition. They carefully examined Scott's efforts to expand the FLVS, increase the use of eTests, and increase adoptions of eTextbooks. Although they had reservations about all three initiatives, they were convinced that the eTests and eTextbooks would be especially disruptive. They therefore concentrated on them.

The parents made it clear that they objected to the manner in which eTests and eTextbooks were being implemented. They predicted that both initiatives would flounder because they were not accompanied by the funds to hire technically savvy staff, upgrade computer hardware, purchase recent software, and acquire high-speed Internet services (Carr, 2011; Thompson, 2017).

Scott became annoyed at the recalcitrant parents. He adopted a tough-guy demeanor. He warned them that he would deal with them by penalizing the schools that their children attended. He assumed that they would flinch. He was shocked when they did not.

Scott soon regretted his face-off with the parents. He was contemplating a run for the U.S. Senate. He feared that the parental incident would disrupt his campaign.

Scott was willing to partially mollify the parents. He told them that he would be delaying his directive to use more eTests. However, he made it clear that he would not be delaying his directive to use more eTextbooks (Giordano, 2015, 2016; Larrabee, 2017a; Mencimer, 2014).

Do Floridians Have the Right Idea about Textbooks? 69

RESPONDING TO PUBLIC QUESTIONS

Florida's politicians were pressured to change some of their regulations. They were urged to loosen their sales regulations for liquor but tighten their purchasing regulations for textbooks.

Activity 8.1

Florida's legislators strictly regulated alcohol. They historically had forbidden supermarkets, drugstores, and gas stations from selling distilled spirits. How did groups respond?

Table 8.1 identifies two groups: liquor store owners and consumers.

Complete the table by indicating the ways in which the groups responded to the legislators. You can use symbols.

Use the symbol – if the groups expressed low confidence in them. Use the symbol ± for moderate confidence and the symbol + for high confidence. As a final step, explain the basis for the symbols that you selected.

You can rely on the information in this chapter, additional information, or the information cited in the references. If you are reading this chapter with colleagues, you can confer with them.

Table 8.1. Florida's Legislators Strictly Regulate Liquor Sales

Groups	Response*	Explanation
Owners—Liquor Stores		
Consumers		

* – Low
  ± Moderate
  + High

Activity 8.2

Some of Florida's legislators pledged to loosen their alcohol regulations. They wished to permit supermarkets, drug stores, and gas stations to sell distilled spirits. How did the groups respond?

Table 8.2 identifies two groups: liquor store owners and consumers.

Complete the table by indicating the ways in which the groups responded to the legislators. You can use symbols.

70 Chapter Eight

Use the symbol – if the groups expressed low confidence in them. Use the symbol ± for moderate confidence and the symbol + for high confidence. As a final step, explain the basis for the symbols that you selected.

Table 8.2. Legislators Pledge to Loosen Liquor Sales Regulations

Groups	Response*	Explanation
Owners—Liquor Stores		
Consumers		

* – Low
± Moderate
+ High

Activity 8.3

Florida's governors had not strictly regulated textbooks. They historically had not pressured schools to purchase digital editions. How did groups respond?

Table 8.3 identifies two groups: scholastic publishers and parents.

Complete the table by indicating the ways in which the groups responded to the governors. You can use symbols.

Use the symbol – if the groups expressed low confidence in them. Use the symbol ± for moderate confidence and the symbol + for high confidence. As a final step, explain the basis for the symbols that you selected.

Table 8.3. Florida's Governors Loosely Regulate Textbook Purchases

Groups	Response*	Explanation
Publishers		
Parents		

* – Low
± Moderate
+ High

Activity 8.4

Governor Rick Scott promised to tighten Florida's textbook regulations. He pressured schools to purchase more digital editions. How did the groups respond?

Table 8.4 identifies two groups: scholastic publishers and parents.

Complete the table by indicating the ways in which these groups responded to the governor. You can use symbols.

Use the symbol – if the groups expressed low confidence in him. Use the symbol ± for moderate confidence and the symbol + for high confidence. As a final step, explain the basis for the symbols that you selected.

Table 8.4. A Governor Pledges to Tighten Textbook Purchasing Regulations

Groups	Response*	Explanation
Publishers		
Parents		

* – Low
± Moderate
+ High

SUMMARY

Florida's politicians were pressured to change their regulations. They were urged to loosen the sales regulations for liquor but tighten the purchasing regulations for textbooks.

Chapter Nine

Do Superintendents Have the Right Idea about Textbooks?

[Even though we agreed to buy commercial in-print textbooks] at an earlier meeting, [we are] making a change. —Duval School Board minutes, 2015

[The school board] will switch from [commercial in-print] textbooks to online printouts. —Journalist Denise Amos, 2015

[The school board made this switch after it] began to think more out-of-the-box. —Superintendent Nikolai Vitti, quoted by Steiner & Vitti, 2016

Do you agree with [the local school board's] decision to switch from [commercial in-print] textbooks to online printouts? —High school English teacher Shannon Russell, 2015

Chrysler dealers historically had reported precise information about vehicle sales. A Florida superintendent had followed the same practice for textbook purchasing. However, they wondered whether they would benefit more from less precise reporting.

REPORTING ABOUT AUTO SALES

The Chrysler Corporation had once been an automotive giant. It had tens of thousands of workers, multiple factories, and hundreds of auto dealerships ("Ford Tops GM," 2015; "Ford, GM, Chrysler," 2015; "Number of General Motors," 2017).

Chrysler eventually became less prosperous. In fact, it declined to the point that it was in genuine peril.

Chrysler's executives went to President George W. Bush. They told him that were on the verge of laying off workers, shutting down plants, and closing dealerships. They then requested federal assistance to avoid these consequences.

Bush asked the executives how much they would require. They responded that they and General Motors, which was another financially beleaguered auto firm, needed seventeen billion dollars. They intended to split the amount.

Bush agreed to give the executives the money they had requested. However, he stipulated that they develop a plan for repaying it (Allen & Rogers, 2008).

The executives accepted the president's terms. They were confident that their corporations could recover. They would furnish monthly sales figures to demonstrate that they were on the right track.

Chrysler's executives expected the sales figures to increase as a result of the government loan. They were upset when they did not. They panicked when sales continued to decline.

Chrysler's executives wished that they had requested more money. They contacted their colleagues at General Motors, who stated that they also should have asked for more money.

The executives arranged another presidential meeting. Since Bush was no longer in office, they had to deal with Obama. They explained to him that the previous federal loan had been insufficient to keep their workers employed, plants open, and dealerships operating.

Obama wanted to know how much more the executives needed. They replied that they required an additional sixty billion dollars.

Obama was willing to provide another loan. However, he set the same condition that Bush had set for the previous one: The executives would have to develop a plan for repaying it.

The executives accepted these terms. After they had received the money, they used monthly sales figures to demonstrate that they were recovering. They compiled these figures from reports that their dealers supplied to them (Laing, 2015).

Enthusiasts

The executives at Chrysler were sure that sales figures would rise as a result of the second loan. They anticipated that the politicians who had backed the loan would then take credit for rescuing the domestic automobile industry and its workers.

The Chrysler executives were concerned about consumers as well as politicians. They hoped that rising sales figures would convince consumers that their firm would continue to create vehicles, stand behind them, and regain its former stature.

The executives were concerned about one more group—journalists. They cared about them because they disseminated monthly sales figures and editorialized about their significance. They did not underestimate the influence that they had on investors and consumers (*New York Times* Editorial Board, 2016b August 2; "Sales and Share," 2017).

Skeptics

The journalists were interested in both General Motors and Chrysler. However, they noted that General Motors had claimed to be struggling, while Chrysler had stated that it was headed for a meltdown. They wondered whether Chrysler would be able to avoid that catastrophic fate.

Chrysler continued to have serious problems. In fact, it was forced to merge with Fiat, an overseas manufacturer. After that union, it adopted a new name—Fiat Chrysler Automobiles (FCA).

Before the merger, Chrysler had been reporting the number of vehicles that their dealers were selling off their lots. Afterward, it continued to make these reports. However, it began to supply conglomerate figures for all FCA vehicles that their dealers sold.

The journalists began reviewing the conglomerate figures. They were not surprised by the figures themselves. However, they were surprised at the rate at which they grew each month (Cost, 2014; Gerdes, 2013; Laing, 2015).

The journalists initially attributed the growing sales figures to the government loan and the corporate merger. However, they became more skeptical after this growth continued for years.

The journalists decided to examine the auto firm in greater detail. They focused their attention on its dealers (Vlasic & Boudette, 2016).

The FCA dealers had been receiving cash incentives for the new vehicles that they sold. However, some of them had devised a way to compound those incentives: They were purchasing vehicles from their own lots, pocketing the cash incentives, and then clandestinely reselling the vehicles at independent lots (Snavely, 2016).

The executives realized that the dealers were benefiting from their shenanigans. However, they acknowledged that the entire corporation was benefiting as well. For this second reason, they did not object (Snavely & Gardner, 2016).

The executives later changed their stance toward their dealers. They were forced to take this step after the Security Exchange Commission revealed that it was investigating the firm for its reporting practices (Ingrassia, 2011; Greenberg, 2012; Noskova, 2016).

REPORTING ABOUT TEXTBOOK PURCHASING

Early entrepreneurs were excited about textbooks. They relied on a five-step formula to produce them. They printed them on paper, sandwiched them between sturdy covers, bound them, and stored them in warehouses.

The entrepreneurs who sold in-print textbooks were extremely successful. Some of them expanded into large corporations with tens of thousands of clients. They eventually were selling hundreds of millions of textbooks (Giordano, 2003).

The executives who managed the large publishing corporations never lost confidence in their in-print textbooks. Nonetheless, they became increasingly intrigued by eTextbooks.

The executives discerned some clear benefits to eTextbooks. They noted that they did not require paper, binding, covers, warehousing, or shipping. They were certain that profits from them would be even greater than those from in-print textbooks (Giordano, 2015).

The corporate executives knew that their production expenses for eTextbooks would be lower than for in-print textbooks. As a result, they could set lower prices for them. They hoped that this feature would persuade clients to purchase them. They directed their sales teams to contact clients and highlight the lower prices.

The sales teams realized that superintendents had an enormous influence on textbook purchases. They made sure to meet with them.

The sales teams urged the superintendents to purchase eTextbooks because of the money that they would save. However, they gave them another important reason to purchase them.

The sales teams told the superintendents that the nation was shifting from in-print textbooks to eTextbooks. They confided that they had the chance to become leaders in this shift.

The sales teams noted that Apple and IBM had been preparing for this shift by investing heavily in digital scholastic materials. They added that the U.S. Office of Education had been preparing by reducing the amount of funds that it provided for in-print materials and increasing the amount for digital materials (Giordano, 2012, 2015, 2016; Harris, 2016; Singer, 2016).

The sales teams were pleased with those superintendents who shared this information within their school districts and then purchased eTextbooks. They were annoyed at those who hesitated.

The sales teams supplied the laggard superintendents with additional information: They gave them sales figures for digital materials. However, they gave them conglomerate sales figures for all digital materials, trade books as well as textbooks. They claimed that these figures, which were rising, comprised additional evidence of the shift from printed to digital textbooks (Fallon, 2014).

Enthusiasts

The sales teams met personally with as many superintendents as they could. They concentrated on those who were appointed to districts with numerous students and large textbook budgets. They made sure to visit the superintendent in Jacksonville, Florida.

Nikolai Vitti was Jacksonville's superintendent in 2015. He regularly supplied his school board members with precise figures for recent textbook purchases. He then recommended how much they should spend for future purchases. He suggested that they spend thirteen million dollars on new textbooks in that year (Gancarski, 2015).

Vitti obtained the thirteen million dollars he had requested for textbooks. Nonetheless, he was annoyed that he was about to spend so much. He wished to spend significantly less.

Vitti went back and reexamined the information that he had received from the sales teams. He noted that school districts were saving some money by switching to commercial eTextbooks. Nonetheless, he did not think that his own district would save a significant amount of money by making this shift.

Vitti needed a bold plan to cut textbook expenditures significantly. He eventually came up with one.

When Vitti revealed his plan, he surprised the publishers with whom he had been in contact. He surprised everyone in Jacksonville as well.

Vitti recommended that the district cease purchasing in-print textbooks from commercial publishers. He added that it also should avoid eTextbooks from those publishers. He identified a government-funded website from which the district could download free teacher-crafted materials instead (Amos 2016a; "Duval Schools Switch," 2015).

Skeptics

Vitti presented his plan to the school board members. He intended to sequester the money that they had allocated for in-print textbooks and reallocate it for other purposes. He was pleased after they gave him permission.

Vitti still had to present his plan to teachers. He told them that they would be switching from traditional textbooks to online materials. He stated that

78   Chapter Nine

they should be enthusiastic because this switch would place them at the forefront of a digital revolution in education. He then waited to see how they would react.

The teachers were skeptical of the plan. They anticipated practical problems using digital materials. They explained that they lacked appropriate computers, Internet service, software, and technical assistance (Amos, 2015; 2016a; 2016b; 2016c).

Vitti told the teachers to be resourceful. He explained that they could locate suitable computers somewhere in the district, use them to search for online learning materials, and then print copies of those materials. He encouraged them to run off enough copies for the students in all of their classes (Amos, 2015).

The teachers were still skeptical. They calculated that district-wide printing of instructional materials would require thousands of labor hours and millions of funding dollars (*"Times Union* Believes," 2015).

Vitti did not have a strategy to cover the labor. However, he did have one to cover the cost. He would reallocate three million dollars from the money originally budgeted for in-print textbooks (Amos, 2015; Steiner & Vitti, 2016).

Some of the teachers remained skeptical. They were able to round up parents who had similar doubts. Together, they created a commotion in the community (Amos, 2016b, 2016c, 2016d; "EngageNY Duval's New Reading," 2015).

POSING QUESTIONS ABOUT MISLEADING INFORMATION

Chrysler dealers historically had reported precise information about vehicle sales. A superintendent had followed the same practice for textbook purchasing. However, they wondered whether they would benefit more from less precise reports.

Activity 9.1

Chrysler dealers had historically provided precise sales reports. How did groups respond?

Table 9.1 identifies two groups: corporate investors and automobile consumers.

Complete the table by indicating the ways in which the groups responded to the dealers. You can use symbols.

Use the symbol – if the groups expressed low confidence in them. Use the symbol ± for moderate confidence and the symbol + for high confidence. As a final step, explain the basis for the symbols that you selected.

Do Superintendents Have the Right Idea about Textbooks? 79

You can rely on the information in this chapter, additional information, or the information cited in the references. If you are reading this chapter with colleagues, you can confer with them.

Table 9.1. Auto Dealers Provide Precise Sales Reports

Groups	Response*	Explanation
Investors		
Consumers		

* – Low
± Moderate
+ High

Activity 9.2

After they were receiving cash incentives for the vehicles that they sold, the dealers provided less precise sales reports. How did the groups respond?

Table 9.2 identifies two groups: corporate investors and automobile consumers.

Complete the table by indicating the ways in which the groups responded to the dealers. You can use symbols.

Use the symbol – if the groups expressed low confidence in them. Use the symbol ± for moderate confidence and the symbol + for high confidence. As a final step, explain the basis for the symbols that you selected.

Table 9.2. Dealers Provide Less Precise Sales Reports

Groups	Response*	Explanation
Investors		
Consumers		

* – Low
± Moderate
+ High

Activity 9.3

Superintendent Vitti provided precise reports about textbook purchasing. How did groups respond?

Table 9.3 identifies two local groups: teachers and parents with children in the schools.

Complete the table by indicating the ways in which the groups responded to the superintendent. You can use symbols.

Use the symbol – if the groups expressed low confidence in him. Use the symbol ± for moderate confidence and the symbol + for high confidence. As a final step, explain the basis for the symbols that you selected.

Table 9.3. A Florida Superintendent Provides Precise Reports about Textbook Purchasing

Groups	Response*	Explanation
Teachers		
Parents		

* – Low
  ± Moderate
  + High

Activity 9.4

After he had access to free online classroom materials, the superintendent provided less precise reports about textbook purchasing. How did the groups respond?

Table 9.4 identifies two local groups: teachers and parents with children in the schools.

Complete the table by indicating the ways in which the groups responded to the superintendent. You can use symbols.

Use the symbol – if the groups expressed low confidence in him. Use the symbol ± for moderate confidence and the symbol + for high confidence. As a final step, explain the basis for the symbols that you selected.

Table 9.4. The Superintendent Provides Less Precise Reports about Textbook Purchasing

Groups	Response*	Explanation
Teachers		
Parents		

* – Low
  ± Moderate
  + High

SUMMARY

Chrysler dealers historically had reported precise information about vehicle sales. A Florida superintendent had followed the same practice for textbook purchasing. In both cases, they wondered whether they would benefit more from less precise reports.

Chapter Ten

Do Journalists Have the Right Idea about Textbooks?

[Teachers unions have a] monopoly hold on taxpayers and children. —*Wall Street Journal* Editorial Board, 2016c

[Teachers unions have] protected perverts, drunkards and other classroom miscreants. —*Wall Street Journal* Editorial Board, 2017h

Teachers unions . . . benefit labor at the expense of students. —*Wall Street Journal* Editorial Board, 2018

Democrats do whatever the teachers unions tell them. —*Wall Street Journal* Editorial Board, 2017a

A university president was upset with his critics. He expected the student journalists on his campus to help him discredit them. Textbook publishers, who were upset with their critics, expected help from professional journalists.

EXAMINING UNIVERSITIES

Bill Clinton had impressive political skills. He demonstrated them in several state and presidential campaigns.

Fifteen years after he retired from office, Clinton still was using his political skills. However, he was using them to help his spouse campaign for president.

When the former president was quizzed about the advice that he was giving to Hillary Clinton, he responded candidly. He had urged her to develop a convincing narrative about her qualifications for office. He expected her to unveil details of that narrative in speeches and ads (Chozick, 2015).

Although Bill Clinton knew that some journalists would echo Hillary Clinton's narrative, he was sure that others would offer an alternative one. He warned that these diverging narratives would make it "very hard for the American people to be well informed" (Bill Clinton, quoted by Chozick, 2015).

Members of the public may have been enlightened by Bill Clinton's insights about campaign narratives. However, professional journalists were already aware of the importance of these narratives. In fact, they were developing narratives to help some candidates and discredit others (Goldberg, 2016; McArdle, 2011; Payan, 2016).

Enthusiasts

Journalists were always on the lookout for stories about political leaders. They knew that their audiences would be interested in them. However, they suspected that they would be interested in stories about other leaders, including those at universities.

The journalists searched for unusual university-based incidents. They became fascinated by those at a small school in rural Maryland.

Mount Saint Mary's University had been established in 1808. Although some persons identified it by its full name, most referred to it simply as "the Mount."

The Mount was a training site for Roman Catholic priests. Because of this specialized mission, it could attract a limited number of students. It struggled to remain in operation.

The trustees had tried to solve the Mount's fiscal problems. However, they had made little progress. They were convinced that they needed a dynamic leader. They were excited when Simon Newman, a financial executive, applied for their presidential position.

Newman was poised, professional, and confident. He promised to increase the school's endowment, refurbish its brand, revamp its business operations, and expand its student body. He contended that his entrepreneurial experiences had prepared him to accomplish these goals (Newman, 2016).

The trustees were entranced by Newman. They enthusiastically hired him.

Skeptics

Newman was eager to tackle some of the Mount's practical problems. He quickly identified one: The school had too many weak students.

Newman blamed the Mount's professors for weak students. Although he acknowledged that they had not recruited them, he contended that they had exacerbated their situation by treating them as if they were "cuddly bunnies."

Newman told his professors to quit cuddling students. He suggested that they instead "put a Glock" to their heads (DeJesus, 2016).

The professors were shocked by their president's rhetoric. However, they were more shocked by the plan he had in mind: he wished to dismiss some students during their first year at the school (Schisler & Golden, 2016).

The professors wished to block their president. However, they needed allies. They therefore went to student journalists and told them about the president's plan. The professors hoped that the student journalists would publicize it. They beamed when the student journalists complied (Golden, 2016).

Newman was upset by the report in the campus newspaper. He was particularly upset by the narrative that it employed. It depicted him as an ambitious executive who was trying to advance his career at the students' expense.

Newman countered with his own narrative. He stated that he had been hired to make the Mount financially stable. He insisted that he was taking the appropriate steps to achieve this goal (Newman, 2016).

Newman waited to see how the student journalists would respond to his narrative. He hoped that they would withdraw their support from his critics and shift it to him. He was disappointed when they did not. He therefore devised a new narrative.

Newman stated that the campus was in an unprecedented state of turmoil. He blamed the situation on the professors who had leaked his plan. He intended to restore calm by summarily dismissing them (Korn, 2016b, 2016d).

Newman expected the student journalists to sympathize with his new narrative. He was disappointed when they did not. They refused to incorporate that narrative into their own reporting.

Newman concluded that he could not handle the student journalists on his own. He asked the chairman of the board of trustees to come to his aid.

The chairman was eager to help. He penned a letter and demanded that the student journalists publish it. In that letter, he stated that President Newman had been correct to attribute the Mount's financial problems to weak students. He added that he also had been correct to attribute the discord on campus to disloyal professors. He commended the manner in which he was handling both situations (Coyne, 2016).

Newman expected the student journalists to cease their resistance. However, he soon realized that he had been too optimistic.

The student journalists contacted their professional peers at prominent news organizations. They told them about the campus commotion. They hoped that they would share this information with a national audience.

When Newman learned that professional journalists were getting involved, he was excited. He expected them to reinforce his narrative and discredit that of his critics.

The professional journalists described the president's difficulties. However, they exhibited little interest in the narratives that he had constructed to explain them. They instead focused on the narratives from his critics (Joseph & McPhate, 2016; Lukianoff, 2017; Stack, 2016; Svrluga, 2016).

EXAMINING TEXTBOOKS

Businesspeople depended on the schools to purchase their products. However, those who sold textbooks had a special type of dependence. After all, the schools were their only clients.

The textbook publishers hired sales teams to visit the schools and meet with administrators and teachers. They hoped that they would convince the school personnel to purchase products from their firms rather than from rival firms.

The textbook publishers were not satisfied after their sales teams had contacted educators. They wished to contact another influential group—politicians. They therefore hired government lobbyists. They hoped that they would convince the politicians to purchase their products.

The lobbyists concentrated on politicians in states with large school budgets. For example, they contacted George W. Bush when he was the governor of Texas. They requested that he link their textbooks to state-mandated tests. They later contacted his brother in Florida and made the same request (Giordano, 2016).

Enthusiasts

The publishers were excited about the politicians whom they were recruiting as allies. They did not underestimate their influence on sales. Nonetheless, they still had to deal with powerful opponents, many of whom were teachers.

The textbook publishers concluded that they would need more troops to successfully take on the teachers. They went to the editors of the *Wall Street Journal* (*WSJ*).

The textbook publishers had gone to the *WSJ* editors in the past. They had been pleased by the manner in which they had helped promote products. They now wanted them to help handle the opponents of those products. They identified teachers as their most troublesome opponents (Giordano, 2003, 2004, 2005, 2012a; 2016, 2017).

The editors were willing to help. They had been waging a decades-long campaign against unionized laborers in industry, retail, and commerce. They were excited by the chance to expand that campaign to unionized teachers.

The editors had good reasons to attack unionized teachers. They resented the "monopoly hold" they had on the schools and the way that they used it to keep out entrepreneurs (*Wall Street Journal* Editorial Board, 2016c).

The editors released a torrent of writing against unionized teachers. They repeatedly castigated them for caring more about their salaries than their students (*Wall Street Journal* Editorial Board, 2017a; 2017b; 2017c; 2017d; 2017e; 2017f; 2017g; 2017h; 2017i; 2017j; 2018).

The editors lambasted not just unionized teachers but any politicians who sympathized with them. They complained that these politicians, who were mostly Democrats, were collaborating with unions in order to gain campaign endorsements, cash, and votes (*Wall Street Journal* Editorial Board, 2015a, 2015b, 2016a, 2017c).

The editors wondered how their regular readers were reacting to this aggressive style of writing. They recalled how enthusiastic they had been when they had used it against unionized laborers in commerce, industry, and retailing. They believed that they would be just as enthusiastic about attacks against unionized teachers. They were correct.

Skeptics

Not everyone was pleased by the *WSJ*'s editorials. Teachers were understandably unhappy. Nonetheless, few of them countered with letters to the editor. They may have assumed that they would have little chance of being published.

Some politicians also were unhappy about the *WSJ*'s editorials. Democrats who had received support from teachers unions were perturbed.

The *WSJ* editors were not surprised by the way that teachers and Democratic politicians were reacting to their editorials. However, they wondered about parents. They realized that parents historically had refused to blame teachers for the problems in the schools. They hoped that their editorials had made them change that stance.

The editors wanted to see parents become less sympathetic to teachers and more sympathetic to entrepreneurs. They were disappointed after they detected few signs of that shift (Giordano, 2009, 2014, 2015, 2016, 2017).

POSING QUESTIONS ABOUT CONTROVERSIAL NARRATIVES

When a university president made controversial recommendations for his campus, he tried to win over student journalists. When textbook publishers made controversial recommendations for the public schools, they tried to win over professional journalists.

Activity 10.1

The president of Mount Saint Mary's University called for controversial changes on his campus. How did groups respond?

Table 10.1 identifies two campus groups: the trustees and student journalists.

Complete the table by indicating the ways in which the groups responded to the president. You can use symbols.

Use the symbol – if the groups expressed low confidence in him. Use the symbol ± for moderate confidence and the symbol + for high confidence. As a final step, explain the basis for the symbols that you selected.

You can rely on the information in this chapter, additional information, or the information cited in the references. If you are reading this chapter with colleagues, you can confer with them.

Table 10.1. A University President Makes Controversial Recommendations

Groups	Response*	Explanation
Trustees		
Student Journalists		

* – Low
  ± Moderate
  + High

Activity 10.2

The president was upset when persons criticized his recommendations. He reached out for allies. How did the groups respond?

Table 10.2 identifies two campus groups: the trustees and student journalists.

Complete the table by indicating the ways in which the groups responded to the president. You can use symbols.

Use the symbol – if the groups expressed low confidence in him. Use the symbol ± for moderate confidence and the symbol + for high confidence. As a final step, explain the basis for the symbols that you selected.

Table 10.2. The President Reaches Out for Allies

Groups	Response*	Explanation
Trustees		
Student Journalists		

* – Low
± Moderate
+ High

Activity 10.3

Textbook publishers made controversial recommendations for the public schools. How did groups respond?

Table 10.3 identifies two groups: editors at the *Wall Street Journal* and parents.

Complete the table by indicating the ways in which the groups responded to the publishers. You can use symbols.

Use the symbol – if the groups expressed low confidence in them. Use the symbol ± for moderate confidence and the symbol + for high confidence. As a final step, explain the basis for the symbols that you selected.

Table 10.3. Textbook Publishers Make Controversial Recommendations

Groups	Response*	Explanation
Editors—WSJ		
Parents		

* – Low
± Moderate
+ High

Activity 10.4

The textbook publishers were upset when persons criticized their recommendations. They reached out for help. How did the groups respond?

Table 10.4 identifies two groups: editors at the *Wall Street Journal* and parents.

Complete the table by indicating the ways in which the groups responded to the publishers. You can use symbols.

Use the symbol – if the groups expressed low confidence in them. Use the symbol ± for moderate confidence and the symbol + for high confidence. As a final step, explain the basis for the symbols that you selected.

Table 10.4. The Publishers Reach Out for Allies

Groups	Response*	Explanation
Editors—*WSJ*		
Parents		

* – Low
± Moderate
+ High

SUMMARY

A university president made controversial recommendations for his campus; he hoped that student journalists would side with him instead of his critics. Textbook publishers made controversial recommendations for the public schools; they hoped that professional journalists would side with them instead of their critics.

References

Actions of the 82nd Legislature. (2017). Texas Historical Association/University of Texas at Austin. Retrieved from: http://texasalmanac.com/topics/education/recent-changes-public-schools.

Allen, G. (2017, July 31). New Florida law lets residents challenge school textbooks. *Wisconsin Public Radio*. Retrieved from: https://www.wpr.org/new-florida-law-lets-residents-challenge-school-textbooks.

Allen, M., & Rogers, D. (2008, December 19). Bush announces $17.4 billion auto bailout. *Politico*. Retrieved from: http://www.politico.com/story/2008/12/bush-announces-174-billion-auto-bailout-016740.

Amend Florida SB 864 so that all counties are REQUIRED to create an instructional materials committee. (2017). Change.org. Retrieved from: https://www.change.org/p/florida-governor-amend-florida-sb-864-so-that-all-counties-are-required-to-create-an-instructional-materials-committee.

Amos, D. S. (2015, June 24). Duval schools will switch from textbooks to online printouts for elementary math, reading next year. *Florida Times-Union*. Retrieved from: http://jacksonville.com/news/metro/2015-06-22/story/duval-schools-will-switch-textbooks-online-printouts-elementary-math.

Amos, D. S. (2016a, January 15). Teacher pleads for more flexibility, creativity in Duval classrooms. *Florida Times-Union*. Retrieved from: http://jacksonville.com/news/metro/2016-01-15/story/teacher-pleads-more-flexibility-creativity-duval-classrooms.

Amos, D. S. (2016b, April 8). Duval schools to bring math, reading books back to elementary schools. *Florida Times-Union*. Retrieved from: http://jacksonville.com/news/metro/2016-04-08/story/duval-schools-bring-math-reading-books-back-elementary-schools.

Amos, D. S. (2016c, June 21). Duval school board member resigns to run for state house seat. *Florida Times-Union*. Retrieved from: http://jacksonville.com/news/metro/2016-06-21/story/duval-school-board-member-resigns-run-state-house-seat.

Amos, D. S. (2016d, August 12). School board District 7 race pits 4 educators against 2 businessmen. *Florida Times-Union*. Retrieved from: http://jacksonville.com/news/metro/2016-08-11/story/school-board-district-7-race-pits-4-educators-against-2-businessmen.

Annenberg Public Policy Center. (2014, September 17). Americans know surprisingly little about their government, survey finds. Author. Retrieved from: http://www.annenbergpublicpolicycenter.org/americans-know-surprisingly-little-about-their-government-survey-finds.

Arnold, K. (2016, December 26). Big-box retailers fight to tear down liquor-store walls. *Orlando Sentinel*. Retrieved from: http://www.orlandosentinel.com/business/consumer/os-liquor-stores-grocery-wall-20151226-story.html.

Auric, P. (2017, January 10). 10 dangers of self-driving cars. Wallst.com. Retrieved from: http://247wallst.com/autos/2017/01/10/10-dangers-of-self-driving-cars.

Austin, N. (2016, July 19). Reframing history: Lessons dip deeper into the well. *Modesto Bee*. Retrieved from: http://www.modbee.com/news/local/education/nan-austin/article90669062.html.

Band, J. (2013, November 21). The changing textbook industry. Project-disco.org. Retrieved from: http://www.project-disco.org/competition/112113-the-changing-textbook-industry/#.V_ecE2cVCpo.

Barrow, D. (2016, January 21). Don't blame Common Core for publishers' lousy textbooks. Edexcellence.net. Retrieved from: https://edexcellence.net/articles/dont-blame-common-core-for-publishers-lousy-textbooks.

Beall, J. (2012, September 12). Predatory publishers are corrupting open access. *Nature*. Retrieved from: http://www.nature.com/news/predatory-publishers-are-corrupting-open-access-1.11385.

Beechhold, H. F. (1971). *The creative classroom: Teaching without textbooks*. New York: Scribner.

Bellafante, G. (2017, February 10). Reaction in New York to Betsy DeVos: A lot of shrugs. *New York Times*. Retrieved from: https://www.nytimes.com/2017/02/10/nyregion/betsy-devos-education-trump.html.

Berlatsky, N. (Ed.). (2012). *Are textbooks biased?* Farmington Hills, MI: Greenhaven.

Berry, S. (2014, December 6). Jeb Bush's "education reform" empire. Breitbart.com. Retrieved from: http://www.breitbart.com/big-government/2014/12/06/jeb-bush-s-education-reform-empire.

Berry, S. (2016, January 21). Exclusive: Former Pearson exec reveals anti-American agenda in Common Core. Breitbart.com. Retrieved from: http://www.breitbart.com/big-government/2016/01/21/exclusive-former-pearson-exec-reveals-anti-american-agenda-in-common-core-on-constitution-guns-christianity.

Bhagwat, A. (2016, May 4). Banning trademarks called offensive violates free speech. *New York Times*. Retrieved from: http://www.nytimes.com/roomfordebate/2016/05/04/redskins-and-other-troubling-trademarks.

Bishop, R. (2005). *Intelligent vehicle technology and trends*. Boston: Artech.

Bizon, N., Dascalescu, L., & Mahdavi, T. N. (2014). *Autonomous vehicles: Intelligent transport systems and smart technologies*. Hauppauge, New York: Nova Science.

Blake, M. (2010, January/February). Revisionaries: How a group of Texas conservatives is rewriting your kids' textbooks. *Washington Monthly*. Retrieved from: http://www.washingtonmonthly.com/features/2010/1001.blake.html.

Blue, M. (2014, November 21). Texas approves textbooks with Moses as honorary founding father. Rightwingwatch.org. Retrieved from: http://www.rightwingwatch.org/post/texas-approves-textbooks-with-moses-as-honorary-founding-father.

Boarding School Beak. (2014, November 22). No textbooks? No wonder children aren't learning. *The Telegraph*. Retrieved from: http://www.telegraph.co.uk/education/educationopinion/11244931/No-textbooks-No-wonder-children-arent-learning.html.

Bosch, S., & Henderson, K. (2015, April 23) Whole lotta shakin' goin' on: Periodicals price survey—2015. *Library Journal*. Retrieved from: http://lj.libraryjournal.com/2015/04/publishing/whole-lotta-shakin-goin-on-periodicals-price-survey-2015/#.

Boudette, N. E. (2016, June 4). Things that give self-driving cars headaches. *New York Times*. Retrieved from: https://www.nytimes.com/interactive/2016/06/06/automobiles/autonomous-cars-problems.html.

Brayton, E. (2011, August 16). Strange textbook lawsuit in Florida. Patheos.com. Retrieved from: http://www.patheos.com/blogs/dispatches/2011/08/16/strange-textbook-lawsuit-in-florida.

Britton, B. K., Woodward, A., & Binkley, M. (2012). *Learning from textbooks: Theory and practice*. Hoboken, NJ: Taylor & Francis.

Brody, J. E. (2012, April 23). Heavy backpacks can spell chronic back pain for children. *New York Times*. Retrieved from: http://well.blogs.nytimes.com/2012/04/23/heavy-backpacks-can-spell-chronic-back-pain-for-children.

Brody, L. (2014, December 16). ET high teacher scores bring new scrutiny. *Wall Street Journal*. Retrieved from: https://www.wsj.com/articles/revised-evaluations-give-nyc-teachers-high-marks-1418749022.

Brody, L. (2016, August 22). Education Department urges renewal of Pearson entrance-test contract. *Wall Street Journal*. Retrieved from: http://www.wsj.com/articles/nyc-education-department-urges-renewal-of-pearson-testing-contract-1471917368.

Brody, L. (2017, March 30). Schools shift to free, public-domain curricula. *Wall Street Journal*. Retrieved from: https://www.wsj.com/articles/schools-shift-to-free-public-domain-textbooks-1490897412.

Broussard, M. (2014, July 15). Why poor schools can't win at standardized testing. *Atlantic*. Retrieved from: https://www.theatlantic.com/education/archive/2014/07/why-poor-schools-cant-win-at-standardized-testing/374287.

Bunn, G. C. (2012). *The truth machine: A social history of the lie detector*. Baltimore: Johns Hopkins University Press.

Bush, J. (2013, January). Jeb Bush: Students should have the choice of digital schools. Cnn.com. Retrieved from: http://schoolsofthought.blogs.cnn.com/2013/01/31/jeb-bush-students-should-have-the-choice-of-digital-schools.

California Department of Education. (2016, August 17). Textbook weight in California: Summary of the State Board of Education action. Author. Retrieved from: http://www.cde.ca.gov/ci/cr/cf/txtbkwght.asp.

Call, J. (2017, February 15). Opposition mounts to tearing down the liquor wall. News-press.com. Retrieved from: http://www.news-press.com/story/news/politics/2017/02/15/opposition-mounts-tearing-liquor-wall/97979530.

Carey, K. (2016, December 29). A peek inside the strange world of fake academia. *New York Times*. Retrieved from: http://www.nytimes.com/2016/12/29/upshot/fake-academe-looking-much-like-the-real-thing.html.

Carr, N. (2011, August 5). Schools should beware the e-book bandwagon. *Dallas News*. Retrieved from: http://www.dallasnews.com/opinion/commentary/2011/08/05/nicholas-carr-schools-should-beware-the-e-book-bandwagon.

Cavanagh, S. (2015, June 9). N.Y. "open" education effort draws users nationwide. *Education Week*. Retrieved from: http://www.edweek.org/ew/articles/2015/06/10/ny-open-education-effort-draws-users-nationwide.html.

Chaffey, D. (2012, June 17). The difference between paid, owned and earned media. Smartinsights.com. Retrieved from: http://www.smartinsights.com/digital-marketing-strategy/customer-acquisition-strategy/new-media-options.

Chozick, A. (2015, July 10). Bill Clinton's candid views of the political press. *New York Times*. Retrieved from: http://www.nytimes.com/politics/first-draft/2015/07/10/bill-clintons-candid-views-of-the-political-press.

Clark, K. M. (2017, May 5). "I don't like that school book" Bill gives Florida parents more power to object. *Miami Herald*. Retrieved from: http://www.miamiherald.com/news/politics-government/state-politics/article148857169.html.

Clawson, L. (2015, February 11). Pearson profits, public education suffers. *Daily Kos Labor*. Retrieved from: http://www.dailykos.com/story/2015/2/11/1363597/-Pearson-profits-public-education-suffers.

Collier, K., & Cobler, N. (2016, September 12). Publisher defends controversial Mexican-American studies textbook. *Texas Tribune*. Retrieved from: https://www.texastribune.org/2016/09/12/publisher-defends-controversial-mexican-american-s.

Confessore, N., & Yourish, K. (2016, March 15). Measuring Donald Trump's mammoth advantage in free media. *New York Times*. Retrieved from: http://www.nytimes.com/2016/03/16/upshot/measuring-donald-trumps-mammoth-advantage-in-free-media.html.

Coscarelli, J. (2017, June 19). Why the Slants took a fight over their band name to the Supreme Court. *New York Times*. Retrieved from: https://www.nytimes.com/2017/06/19/arts/music/slants-name-supreme-court-ruling.html.

Cost, J. (2014). *Spoiled rotten: How the politics of patronage corrupted the once noble Democratic Party and now threatens the American republic*. New York: HarperCollins.

Cox, J. W., Clement, S., & Vargas, T. (2016, May 19). New poll finds 9 in 10 Native Americans aren't offended by Redskins name. *Washington Post*. Retrieved from: https://www.washingtonpost.com/local/new-poll-finds-9-in-10-native-americans-arent-offended-by-redskins-name/2016/05/18/3ea11cfa-161a-11e6-924d-838753295f9a_story.html.

Coyne, J. (2016, January 19). Letter to the editor: A Message from John Coyne, Chair—On behalf of the Board of Trustees of Mount St. Mary's University. *Mountain Echo. Retrieved from: http://msmecho.com/2016/01/19/letter-to-the-editor-a-message-from-john-coyne-chair-on-behalf-of-the-board-of-trustees-of-mount-st-marys-university/.

Davis, K. (2014, September 7). Carroll schools budget less on textbooks per student than other districts. *Carroll County Times.* Retrieved from: http://www.carrollcountytimes.com/news/local/ph-cc-school-textbooks-20140905-story.html.

Dear Texas lawmaker. (2009, May 19). Scanned Document—Texas Senate. Senate.texas.gov. Retrieved from: www.senate.texas.gov/cmtes/81/c530/HB4294-NolaWellman.pdf.

DeCiccio, E. (2013, October 10). Battle rages over creationism in Texas schools. *Msnbc.com.* Retrieved from: http://tv.msnbc.com/2013/10/01/battle-rages-over-creationism-in-texas-schools.

DeCourcey, D. (2016, September 7). A textbook filled with racist errors is causing debate in Texas. Attn.com. Retrieved from: http://www.attn.com/stories/11203/texas-public-school-has-mexican-american-textbook-with-racist-errors.

DeJesus, I. (2016, February 11). Scandal at Mount St. Mary's: A Glock, a bad choice of words. Pennlive.com. Retrieved from: http://www.pennlive.com/news/2016/02/mount_st_marys_scandal_simon_n.html.

Douglas-Gabriel, D., & Layton, L. (2016, February 11). Obama announces his intent to nominate John B. King Jr. to officially take the role of education secretary. *Washington Post.* Retrieved from: https://www.washingtonpost.com/news/grade-point/wp/2016/02/11/obama-to-nominate-john-b-king-jr-to-officially-take-the-role-of-education-secretary.

Downes, S. (2016, September 10). Trigger warnings, safe spaces and free speech, too. *New York Times.* Retrieved from: http://www.nytimes.com/2016/09/11/opinion/trigger-warnings-safe-spaces-and-free-speech-too.html.

Dudley, D. (2014/2015, December/January). The driverless car is (almost) here. *AARP Magazine.* Retrieved from: http://www.aarp.org/home-family/personal-technology/info-2014/google-self-driving-car.html.

Dugan, I. J., & Spector, M. (2017, August 24). Tesla's push to build a self-driving car sparked dissent among its engineers. *Wall Street Journal.* Retrieved from: https://www.wsj.com/articles/teslas-push-to-build-a-self-driving-car-sparks-dissent-among-its-engineers-1503593742.

Duval schools switch from textbooks to online printouts. (2015, June 23). *Washington Times.* Retrieved from: http://www.washingtontimes.com/news/2015/jun/23/duval-schools-switch-from-textbooks-to-online-prin.

Duval Schools. (2015, June 12). Special board meeting minutes: Duval County Public Schools. Duvalschools.org. Retrieved from: http://www.google.com/url?sa=t&rct=j&q=&esrc=s&source=web&cd=32&ved=0ahUKEwiv16_v9tjSAhWrv1QKHb7YAe84HhAWCB8wAQ&url=http%3A%2F%2Fagenda.duvalschools.org%2FJune%252016%2C%25202015%2520-%2520Special%2520Board%2520Meeting%2520on%2520Tuesday%2C%2520June%252016%2C%25202015%2FE3B963C4-FF40-40A6-B72B-D8710B8EBC69Minutes.pdf&usg=AFQjCNHy35TbX5zECbcdyftoMHOUR0tPRA&sig2=qnIrt3sjx_olUY5vYNqzCA.

EngageNY Duval's new reading curriculum gets poor reviews. (2015, June 25). Jaxkidsmatter.blogspot.com. Retrieved from: http://jaxkidsmatter.blogspot.com/2015/06/engageny-duvals-new-reading-curriculum.html.

Eskandarian, A. (2012). *Handbook of intelligent vehicles*. London: Springer.

Fallon, C. (2014, October 6). Print books outsold eBooks in first half of 2014. *Huffington Post*. Retrieved from: http://www.huffingtonpost.com/2014/10/06/ebooks-print-books-outsold_n_5940654.html.

Farley, C. H. (2016, May 4). Permit free speech without approving offensive speech. *New York Times*. Retrieved from: http://www.nytimes.com/roomfordebate/2016/05/04/redskins-and-other-troubling-trademarks.

Figueroa, A. (2013, August 6). 8 Things you should know about corporations like Pearson that make huge profits from standardized tests. Alternet.org. Retrieved from: http://www.alternet.org/education/corporations-profit-standardized-tests.

Firozi, P. (2017, February 10). Protesters block DeVos from entering DC school. Thehill.com. Retrieved from: http://thehill.com/homenews/news/318924-devos-blocked-from-entering-dc-school.

Florida Citizens' Alliance. (2017, August 11). Live Interview Fox 35 Orlando: Florida's new textbook law. Author. Retrieved from: http://floridacitizensalliance.com/liberty/live-interview-fox-35-orlando-floridas-new-textbook-law.

Florida Department of Education. (2017). Instructional materials. Author. Retrieved from: http://www.fldoe.org/academics/standards/instructional-materials.

Florida Freedom Council. (2011, May 11). Update on SB 2120. Author. Retrieved from: https://www.meetup.com/de-DE/collier912freedomcouncil/messages/boards/thread/11547141.

Florida legislature passes school textbook bill. (2014, May 1). Miami.cbslocal.com. Retrieved from: http://miami.cbslocal.com/2014/05/01/fla-legislature-passes-school-textbook-bill/.

Florida Legislature's 2011 session winners and losers. (2011, May 7). *Tampa Bay Tribune*. Retrieved from: http://www.tampabay.com/news/politics/gubernatorial/florida-legislatures-2011-session-winners-and-losers/1168420.

Florida parents barred from textbook input. (2011, July 8). Education-curriculum-reform-government-schools.org. Retrieved from: http://education-curriculum-reform-government-schools.org/w/2011/07/florida-parents-barred-from-textbook-input.

Ford tops GM in U.S. factory jobs. (2015, February 15). Autonews.com. Retrieved from: http://www.autonews.com/article/20150215/OEM/302169970/ford-tops-gm-in-u.s.-factory-jobs.

Ford, GM, Chrysler job numbers up since recession. (2015, March 5). Crainsdetroit.com. Retrieved from: http://www.crainsdetroit.com/article/20150302/NEWS/303019996/ford-gm-chrysler-job-numbers-up-since-recession.

Friedersdorf, C. (2015, February 21). Can California textbooks criticize slave traders? *Atlantic*. Retrieved from: http://www.theatlantic.com/politics/archive/2015/02/can-california-textbooks-criticize-slave-traders/385634.

Friedman, W. (2016a, September 7). Trump is king of earned media. Mediapost.com. Retrieved from: http://www.mediapost.com/publications/article/284196/trump-is-king-of-earned-media.html.

Friedman, W. (2016b, December 9). Post-election, Trump's earned media soars. Mediapost.com. Retrieved from: http://www.mediapost.com/publications/article/290729/post-election-trumps-earned-media-soars.html.

Frye v. U.S. (2017). 130 S. Ct. 307. Casebriefs.com. Retrieved from: http://www.casebriefs.com/blog/law/evidence/evidence-keyed-to-fisher/lay-opinions-and-expert-testimony/frye-v-u-s.

Fung, B. (2014, May 28). The future of Google's driverless car is old people. *Washington Post*. Retrieved from: https://www.washingtonpost.com/news/the-switch/wp/2014/05/28/the-future-of-googles-driverless-car-is-old-people.

Gabriel, T. (2011, April 26). Jeb Bush leads broad push for education change with "Florida formula." *New York Times*. Retrieved from: http://www.nytimes.com/2011/04/27/education/27bush.html.

Gancarski, A. G. (2015, July 13). Duval County schools instructional material scrutinized for Islamocentrism. Floridapolitics.com. Retrieved from: http://floridapolitics.com/archives/186447-duval-county-schools-instructional-material-scrutinized-for-islamocentrism.

Gay, R. (2015, November 13). The seduction of safety, on campus and beyond. *New York Times*. Retrieved from: https://www.nytimes.com/2015/11/15/opinion/sunday/the-seduction-of-safety-on-campus-and-beyond.html.

Gelber, D. (2015, June 21). Jeb Bush: He "dumbed down" Florida schools. *Miami Herald*. Retrieved from: http://www.miamiherald.com/opinion/op-ed/article25108849.html#storylink=cpy.

Gerdes, L. I. (2013). *Are government bailouts effective?* Detroit: Greenhaven.

Gewertz, C. (2015, February 18). States ceding power over classroom materials. *Education Week*. Retrieved from: http://www.edweek.org/ew/articles/2015/02/18/states-ceding-power-over-classroom-materials.html.

Giordano, G. (2000). *Twentieth-century reading education: Understanding practices of today in terms of patterns of the past*. London, UK: Elsevier/JAI Press.

Giordano, G. (2003). *Twentieth-century textbook wars: A history of advocacy and opposition*. New York: Peter Lang.

Giordano, G. (2004). *Wartime schools: How World War II changed American education*. New York: Peter Lang.

Giordano, G. (2005). *How testing came to dominate American schools: The history of educational assessment*. New York: Peter Lang.

Giordano, G. (2007). *American special education: A history of early political advocacy*. New York: Peter Lang.

Giordano, G. (2009). *Solving education problems effectively: A guide to using the case method*. Lanham, MD: Rowman & Littlefield.

Giordano, G. (2010). *Cockeyed education: A case method primer*. Lanham, MD: Rowman & Littlefield.

Giordano, G. (2011). *Lopsided school: Case method briefings*. Lanham, MD: Rowman & Littlefield.

Giordano, G. (2012a). *Capping costs: Putting a price tag on school reform*. Lanham, MD: Rowman & Littlefield.

Giordano, G. (2012b). *Teachers go to rehab: Historical and current advice to instructors.* Lanham, MD: Rowman & Littlefield.

Giordano, G. (2014). *Commonsense questions about instruction: The answers can provide essential steps to improvement.* Lanham, MD: Rowman & Littlefield.

Giordano, G. (2015). *Common Sense questions about school administration: The answers can provide essential steps to improvement.* Lanham, MD: Rowman & Littlefield.

Giordano, G. (2016). *Common Sense questions about testing: The answers can provide essential steps to improvement.* Lanham, MD: Rowman & Littlefield.

Giordano, G. (2017). *Common Sense questions about learners: Answers to reveal essential steps to improvement.* Lanham, MD: Rowman & Littlefield.

Goldberg, J. (2016, September 28). Narrative-building has become a political obsession. *National Review.* Retrieved from: http://www.nationalreview.com/article/440469/political-narratives-make-facts-serve-larger-storyline.

Golden, R. (2016, January 19). Editorial statement on the article, "Mount president's attempt to improve retention rate included seeking dismissal of 20-25 first-year students." *Mountain Echo.* Retrieved from: http://msmecho.com/2016/01/19/editorial-statement-on-the-article-mount-presidents-attempt-to-improve-retention-rate-included-seeking-dismissal-of-20-25-first-year-students.

Goldstein, D. (2017, February 3). Betsy DeVos, pick for secretary of education, is the most jeered. *New York Times.* Retrieved from: https://www.nytimes.com/2017/02/03/us/politics/betsy-devos-nominee-education-secretary.html.

Goodman, H. (2017, June 29). New state law will put Florida science teaching under attack. *Palm Beach Post.* Retrieved from: http://opinionzone.blog.palmbeachpost.com/2017/06/29/goodman-new-state-law-will-put-florida-science-teaching-under-attack.

Gordon, J. (2014, April 18). Florida senate passes textbook review legislation. Counterjihadreport.com. Retrieved from: https://counterjihadreport.com/2014/04/18/florida-senate-passes-textbook-review-legislation.

Gorn, E. J. (Ed). (1998). *The McGuffey readers: Selections from the 1879 edition.* Boston, MA: Bedford.

Greenberg, J. (2012, September 6). Did President Obama save the auto industry? Politifact.com. Retrieved from: http://www.politifact.com/truth-o-meter/article/2012/sep/06/did-obama-save-us-automobile-industry.

Guillermo, E. (2016, May 4). Government shouldn't help trademark owners profit from hate. *New York Times.* Retrieved from: http://www.nytimes.com/roomfordebate/2016/05/04/redskins-and-other-troubling-trademarks.

Hamers, L. (2016, December 12). Five challenges for self-driving cars. *Science News.* Retrieved from: https://www.sciencenews.org/article/five-challenges-self-driving-cars.

Hananel, S. (2017, January 15). Asian-American group *The Slants'* trademark case heads to Supreme Court. *Denver Post.* Retrieved from: http://www.denverpost.com/2017/01/15/the-slants-supreme-court-trademark.

Harris, E. A. (2016, September 27). Next target for IBM's Watson: Third-grade math. *New York Times*. Retrieved from: http://www.nytimes.com/2016/09/28/nyregion/ibm-watson-common-core.html.

Hedli, L. (2014, October 12). Why self-driving cars will change retirement. *Wall Street Journal*. Retrieved from: http://www.wsj.com/articles/why-self-driving-cars-will-change-retirement-1413147945.

Higgins, T., & Colias, M. (2017, October 1). Self-driving dilemma: How to pass the wheel between human and robot. *Wall Street Journal*. Retrieved from: https://www.wsj.com/articles/self-driving-dilemma-how-to-pass-the-wheel-between-human-and-robot-1506855613.

Hutchins, R. D. (2016). *Nationalism and history education: Curricula and textbooks in the United States and France*. New York: Taylor & Francis.

Ingrassia, P. (2011). *Crash course: The American automobile industry's road to bankruptcy and bailout . . . and beyond*. New York: Random House.

Is NYSED admitting EngageNY modules are crap? (2014, April 27). Perdidostreetschool.blogspot.com. Retrieved from: http://perdidostreetschool.blogspot.com/2014/04/is-nysed-admitting-engageny-modules-are.html.

Isensee, L. (2015, July 13). How textbooks can teach different versions of history. Npr.org. Retrieved from: http://www.npr.org/sections/ed/2015/07/13/421744763/how-textbooks-can-teach-different-versions-of-history.

Jenkins, H. (2006). *Convergence culture: Where old and new media collide*. New York: New York University Press.

Jervis, R. (2014, November 17). Controversial Texas textbooks headed to classrooms. USA TODAY. Retrieved from: http://www.usatoday.com/story/news/nation/2014/11/17/texas-textbook-inaccuracies/19175311/.

Johnson, D. (2015, March 17). Where is St. Patrick to drive the textbooks from the schools? Squarespace.com. Retrieved from: http://doug-johnson.squarespace.com/blue-skunk-blog/2015/3/17/where-is-st-patrick-to-drive-the-textbooks-from-the-schools.html.

Joseph, Y., & McPhate, M. (2016, February 29). Mount St. Mary's president quits after firings seen as retaliatory. *New York Times*. Retrieved from: http://www.nytimes.com/2016/03/02/us/simon-newman-resigns-as-president-of-mount-st-marys.html.

Kamenetz, A. (2016, April). Pearson's quest to cover the planet in company-run schools. *Wired*. Retrieved from: https://www.wired.com/2016/04/apec-schools.

Kaplan. S. (2017, July 1). New Florida law lets any resident challenge what's taught in science classes. *Washington Post*. Retrieved from: https://www.washingtonpost.com/news/speaking-of-science/wp/2017/07/01/new-florida-law-lets-any-resident-challenge-whats-taught-in-science-classes/?utm_term=.f3e0a95b31b7.

Katy Independent School District. (2016). Katy ISD textbooks frequently asked questions. Author. Retrieved from: www.katyisd.org/Pages/Textbooks-FAQs.aspx.

Katyal, S. (2016, May 4). Trademark officials must distinguish between irony and offense. *New York Times*. Retrieved from: http://www.nytimes.com/roomfordebate/2016/05/04/redskins-and-other-troubling-trademarks.

Keogh, S. (2016, September 19). The dangers of "self-driving" car hype. *Wall Street Journal*. Retrieved from: https://www.wsj.com/articles/the-dangers-of-self-driving-car-hype-1474327725.

Killough, A. (2015, November 2). Jeb Bush's e-book: Rubio, the 2000 recount and emails from mom and dad. Cnn.com. Retrieved from: http://www.cnn.com/2015/11/02/politics/jeb-bush-e-book-email.

Koch, J. V. (2006, September). An economic analysis of textbook pricing and textbook markets [ERIC document]. U.S. Department of Education. Retrieved from: files.eric.ed.gov/fulltext/ED497025.pdf.

Kolata, G. (2013, September 2). Guesses and hype give way to data in study of education. *New York Times*. Retrieved from: http://www.nytimes.com/2013/09/03/science/applying-new-rigor-in-studying-education.html.

Korn, M. (2016a, February 11). Barack Obama to nominate John B. King Jr. as U.S. Education Secretary. *Wall Street Journal*. Retrieved from: https://www.wsj.com/articles/barack-obama-to-nominate-john-b-king-jr-as-u-s-education-secretary-1455232975.

Korn, M. (2016b, February 12). Mount St. Mary's faculty rejects olive branch, calls for president to resign. *Wall Street Journal*. Retrieved from: https://www.wsj.com/articles/mount-st-marys-faculty-rejects-olive-branch-calls-for-president-to-resign-1455324865.

Korn, M. (2016c, February 15). Mount St. Mary's president declines to resign. *Wall Street Journal*. Retrieved from: http://www.wsj.com/articles/mount-st-marys-president-declines-to-resign-1455579954.

Korosec, K. (2016, October 20). 4 reasons why Tesla's autonomous driving announcement matters. *Fortune*. Retrieved from: http://fortune.com/2016/10/20/tesla-self-driving-hardware-matters.

Kurtz, S. (2016, June 1). Will California's leftist k-12 curriculum go national? *National Review*. Retrieved from: http://www.nationalreview.com/corner/436083/will-californias-leftist-k-12-curriculum-go-national.

Laing, K. (2015, January 7). Obama: Auto bailout "was the right thing to do." *The Hill*. Retrieved from: http://thehill.com/policy/transportation/228836-obama-auto-bailout-was-the-right-thing-to-do.

Lambert, F. (2016, October 19). Tesla announces all production cars now have fully self-driving hardware. Electrek.co. Retrieved from: https://electrek.co/2016/10/19/tesla-fully-autonomous-self-driving-car.

Larrabee, B. (2017a, February 16). Proposal aimed at cutting school testing times. *Florida Times-Union*. Retrieved from: http://digital.olivesoftware.com/olive/ODN/FloridaTimesUnion/shared/ShowArticle.aspx?doc=TFTU%2F2017%2F02%2F16&entity=Ar01200&sk=8561C3EE.

Larrabee, B. (2017b, February 28). Testing debate teed up again in Florida Legislature. *Palm Beach Post*. Retrieved from: http://www.palmbeachpost.com/news/state—regional-govt—politics/testing-debate-teed-again-florida-legislature/TPaIcjHd2XcnGnECwQyAnM.

Larrabee, B. (2017c, March 21). State senators ponder direction on school testing. *Florida-Times-Union*. Retrieved from: http://digital.olivesoftware.com/olive/

ODN/FloridaTimesUnion/shared/ShowArticle.aspx?doc=TFTU%2F2017%2F03%2F22&entity=Ar01204&sk=556FCD12.

Layton, L. (2015, January 6). Jeb Bush education foundation played leading role in mixing politics, policy. *Washington Post*. Retrieved from: https://www.washingtonpost.com/local/education/jeb-bush-education-foundation-played-leading-role-in-mixing-politics-policy/2015/01/06/db1db176-903b-11e4-a900-9960214d4cd7_story.html.

Lent, R. C. (2012). *Overcoming textbook fatigue: 21st century tools to revitalize teaching and learning*. Alexandria, VA: Association for Supervision and Curriculum Development.

Lewis, J. (Ed.). (2014). *Forensic document examination: Fundamentals and current trends*. San Diego: Elsevier.

Liptak, A. (2016, May 2). Supreme Court could weigh in on Redskins trademark case. *New York Times*. Retrieved from: https://www.nytimes.com/2016/05/03/us/politics/supreme-court-redskins-trademark-case.html.

Liptak, A. (2017, January 18). Justices appear willing to protect offensive trademarks. *New York Times*. Retrieved from: https://www.nytimes.com/2017/01/18/us/politics/justices-appear-willing-to-protect-offensive-trademarks.html.

Loewen, J. W. (1995). *Lies my teacher told me: Everything your American history textbook got wrong*. New York: New Press.

Loewen, J. W. (2010). *Teaching what really happened: How to avoid the tyranny of textbooks and get students excited about doing history*. New York: Teachers College Press.

Los Angeles Times Editorial Board. (2011, April 8). Gays in textbooks: Best told by historians, not by politicians. *Los Angeles Times*. Retrieved from: http://articles.latimes.com/2011/apr/08/opinion/la-ed-textbook-20110408.

Lukianoff, G. (2017, February 17). The 10 worst colleges for free speech: 2016. *Huffington Post*. Retrieved from: http://www.huffingtonpost.com/greg-lukianoff/the-10-worst-colleges-for_b_9243000.html.

Lusk, J. (2014, March 23). How to define and use paid, owned and earned media. *Huffington Post*. Retrieved from: http://www.huffingtonpost.com/john-lusk/how-to-define-and-use-pai_b_4634005.html.

MacGillis, A. (2015, January 26). Testing time. *New Yorker*. Retrieved from: http://www.newyorker.com/magazine/2015/01/26/testing-time.

Masnick, M. (2011, March 4). The artificially high price of academic journals and how it impacts everyone. Techdirt.com. Retrieved from: https://www.techdirt.com/articles/20110226/17334613288/artificially-high-price-academic-journals-how-it-impacts-everyone.shtml.

Maxwell, B. (2011, May 28). Scott's textbook case of myopia: Three bureaucrats will now review school materials. *Tampa Bay Tribune*. Retrieved from: http://www.tampabay.com/opinion/columns/scotts-textbook-case-of-myopia-three-bureaucrats-will-now-review-school/1172197.

McArdle, M. (2011, August 1). The power of political narrative. *Atlantic*. Retrieved from: https://www.theatlantic.com/politics/archive/2011/08/the-power-of-political-narrative/242905.

McFarland, M. (2017, January 10). The backlash against self-driving cars officially begins. Cnn.com. Retrieved from: http://money.cnn.com/2017/01/10/technology/new-york-self-driving-cars-ridesharing.

Medina, J. (2016, May 4). Debate erupts in California over curriculum on India's history. *New York Times*. Retrieved from: http://www.nytimes.com/2016/05/06/us/debate-erupts-over-californias-india-history-curriculum.html.

Mencimer, S. (2014, September 17). Why Rick Scott Is facing a Tea Party revolt in Florida. *Mother Jones*. Retrieved from: http://www.motherjones.com/politics/2014/09/why-rick-scotts-facing-tea-party-revolt-florida.

Mims, C. (2016, September 25). Self-driving hype doesn't reflect reality. *Wall Street Journal*. Retrieved from: http://www.wsj.com/articles/self-driving-hype-doesnt-reflect-reality-1474821801.

Mirengoff, P. (2016, June 1). California poised to adopt ultra-leftist K-12 history curriculum. Powerlineblog.com. Retrieved from: http://www.powerlineblog.com/archives/2016/06/california-poised-to-adopt-ultra-leftist-k-12-history-curriculum.php.

Monahan, R. (2015, March 31). How Common Core is killing the textbook. *Hechinger Report*. Retrieved from: https://qz.com/373643/how-common-core-is-killing-the-textbook.

Morgenstern, M. (2016, September 18). Daubert v. Frye–A state-by-state comparison. Theexpertinstitute.com. Retrieved from: https://www.theexpertinstitute.com/daubert-v-frye-a-state-by-state-comparison.

Morris, C. (2016, July 21). Why California is teaching its students about the LGBT community. *Atlantic*. Retrieved from: http://www.theatlantic.com/education/archive/2016/07/why-california-is-teaching-its-students-about-the-lgbt-community/492221.

Moynihan, D. P. (2017, January 9). Who's really placing limits on free speech? *New York Times*. Retrieved from: http://www.nytimes.com/2017/01/09/opinion/whos-really-placing-limits-on-free-speech.html.

Mulrooney, L. (2017, February 16). Tearing down the liquor wall: Will "whiskey and Wheaties" bill finally clear the Florida legislature? Cltampa.com. Retrieved from: http://www.cltampa.com/news-views/politics/article/20852421/tearing-down-the-liquor-wall-will-whiskey-and-wheaties-bill-finally-clear-the-florida-legislature.

National Council on Disability. (2015). *Self-driving cars: mapping access to a technology revolution*. Washington, DC: Author.

New York State Education Department. (2017). New York state learning standards and core curriculum. Author. Retrieved from: http://www.p12.nysed.gov/ciai/cores.html.

New York Times Editorial Board. (2016a, November 24). No experience, no problem. *New York Times*. Retrieved from: http://www.nytimes.com/2016/11/24/opinion/no-experience-no-problem.html.

New York Times Editorial Board. (2016b, August 2). As homes and cars go, so goes the economy. *New York Times*. Retrieved from: http://www.nytimes.com/2016/08/02/opinion/as-homes-and-cars-go-so-goes-the-economy.html.

New York Times Editorial Board. (2017a, February 2). Wanted: One Republican with integrity, to defeat Betsy DeVos. *New York Times*. Retrieved from: https://www

.nytimes.com/2017/02/02/opinion/wanted-one-republican-with-integrity-to-defeat-betsy-devos.html.
New York Times Editorial Board. (2017b, February 7). Betsy DeVos teaches the value of ignorance. *New York Times*. Retrieved from: https://www.nytimes.com/2017/02/07/opinion/betsy-devos-teaches-the-value-of-ignorance.html.
Newman, D. (2014, December 3). The role of paid, owned and earned media in your marketing strategy. *Forbes*. Retrieved from: http://www.forbes.com/sites/danielnewman/2014/12/03/the-role-of-paid-owned-and-earned-media-in-your-marketing-strategy/2/#419e122e7dd3.
Newman, S. P. (2016, December 2). Message from President Simon P. Newman [Video]. YouTube. Retrieved from: https://www.youtube.com/watch?v=XbpLj_hKQi8.
Noskova, P. (2016, July 26). Fiat Chrysler to revise reporting amid probe of sales data. *Bloomberg*. Retrieved from: https://www.bloomberg.com/news/articles/2016-07-26/fiat-chrysler-probed-by-u-s-on-sales-data-to-revise-reporting.
Number of General Motors employees between FY 2010 and FY 2016. (2017). Statista.com. Retrieved from: https://www.statista.com/statistics/239843/employees-of-general-motors.
O'Connor, J. (2012, November 27). Florida Education Foundation hosting two-day summit in D.C. Npr.org. Retrieved from: https://stateimpact.npr.org/florida/2012/11/27/florida-education-foundation-hosting-two-day-summit-in-d-c.
Ontario-Montclair School District. (2014). Textbook adoption process. Author. Retrieved from: http://omsd.k12.ca.us/departments/lss/academics/textbook/Pages/default.aspx.
Payan, G. (2016, June 14). Don't tell or believe a single story. *Huffington Post*. Retrieved from: http://www.huffingtonpost.com/gustavo-payan/dont-tell-or-believe-a-single-story_b_10403724.html.
Pearson PLC. (2015). About us. Author. Retrieved from: https://www.pearson.com/about-pearson.html.
Pearson PLC. (2017). Who we are. Author. Retrieved from: https://www.pearson.com/corporate/about-pearson/who-we-are.html.
Pérez-Peña, R., Smith, M., & Saul, S. (2016, August 26). University of Chicago strikes back against campus political correctness. *New York Times*. Retrieved from: http://www.nytimes.com/2016/08/27/us/university-of-chicago-strikes-back-against-campus-political-correctness.html.
Pondiscio, R. (2015, May 29). Common Core's first breakout hit. *U.S. News & World Report*. Retrieved from: http://www.usnews.com/opinion/knowledge-bank/2015/05/29/is-common-core-spurring-a-curriculum-renaissance.
Porter-Magee, K., & McDougald, V. (2015, May 20). EngageNY's ELA curriculum is uncommonly engaging. *Thomas B. Fordham Institute*. Retrieved from: https://edexcellence.net/articles/engagenys-ela-curriculum-is-uncommonly-engaging.
Postal, L. (2017, April 18). Parents may get new way to challenge school textbooks. *Orlando Sentinel*. Retrieved from: http://www.orlandosentinel.com/features/education/school-zone/os-instructional-materials-objections-science-pornography-20170414-story.html.

Preston, B. (2016, January 7). Insurers brace for the self-driving future and fewer accidents. *New York Times*. Retrieved from: http://www.nytimes.com/2016/01/08/automobiles/insurers-brace-for-the-self-driving-future-and-fewer-accidents.html.

Problems backpacks can pose. (2017). Kidshealth.org. Retrieved from: http://kidshealth.org/en/parents/backpack.html.

Ramirez, F. (2016, September 26). Christian nonprofit on a mission to influence what goes in Texas textbooks. *Houston Chronicle*. Retrieved from: http://www.chron.com/news/education/article/Texas-man-gets-60-000-in-donations-to-remove-9289169.php.

Ramsey, M., Inada, M., & Kubota, Y. (2016, January 21). Japan road tests self-driving cars to keep aging motorists mobile. *Washington Post*. Retrieved from: http://www.wsj.com/articles/japan-road-tests-self-driving-cars-to-keep-aging-motorists-mobile-1453357504.

Rapp, D. (2008, November/December). The end of textbooks? Scholastic.com. Retrieved from: http://www.scholastic.com/browse/article.jsp?id=3750551.

Redskins, and other troubling trademarks. (2016, May 4). *New York Times*. Retrieved from: http://www.nytimes.com/roomfordebate/2016/05/04/redskins-and-other-troubling-trademarks.

Reingold, J. (2015, January 21). Everybody hates Pearson. *Fortune*. Retrieved from: http://fortune.com/2015/01/21/everybody-hates-pearson.

Roberts, A. (2016, November 9). Donald Trump is the first earned media president. Clickz.com. Retrieved from: https://www.clickz.com/donald-trump-is-the-first-earned-media-president/107787.

Roberts, R. T., DeCandio, M. J., & Ingersoll, A. (2017). From Frye to Daubert: What you need to know about admitting expert testimony in Florida state courts. Marshalldennehey.com. Retrieved from: http://www.marshalldennehey.com/defense-digest-articles/frye-daubert-what-you-need-know-about-admitting-expert-testimony-florida.

Ross, E. (2017, May 15). Revamped "anti-science" education bills in U.S. find success. *Scientific American*. Retrieved from://www.scientificamerican.com/article/revamped-anti-science-education-bills-in-u-s-find-success.

Rothfeder, J. (2014). *Driving Honda: Inside the world's most innovative car company*. New York: Portfolio.

Russell, S. M. (2015, June 22). Textbooks, or printouts? Surveymonkey.com. Retrieved from: https://www.surveymonkey.com/r/6NHQFTB.

Rutenberg, J. (2016, March 20). The mutual dependence of Donald Trump and the news media. *New York Times*. Retrieved from: http://www.nytimes.com/2016/03/21/business/media/the-mutual-dependence-of-trump-and-the-news-media.html.

Sales and share of total market by manufacturer. (2017, March 1). *Wall Street Journal*. Retrieved from: http://online.wsj.com/mdc/public/page/2_3022-autosales.html

Savage, D. G. (2016, September 29). Supreme Court to decide if offensive names such as "Redskins" and "Slants" can be trademarked. *Los Angeles Times*. Retrieved from: http://www.latimes.com/nation/la-fi-supreme-court-trademarks-20160929-snap-story.html.

Schisler, R., & Golden, R. (2016, January 19). Mount president's attempt to improve retention rate included seeking dismissal of 20–25 first-year students. *Mountain Echo*. Retrieved from: http://msmecho.com/2016/01/19/mount-presidents-attempt-to-improve-retention-rate-included-seeking-dismissal-of-20-25-first-year-students.

Schweikart, L., & Allen, M. (2004). *A patriot's history of the United States: From Columbus's great discovery to the war on terror*. New York: Sentinel.

Simon, C. C. (2016, August 1). Fighting for free speech on America's campuses. *New York Times*. Retrieved from: https://www.nytimes.com/2016/08/07/education/edlife/fire-first-amendment-on-campus-free-speech.html.

Simon, S. (2105, February 10). No profit left behind. *Politico*. Retrieved from: http://www.politico.com/story/2015/02/pearson-education-115026.

Singer, N. (2016, September 12). Apple offers free app to teach children coding (iPads sold separately). *New York Times*. Retrieved from: http://www.nytimes.com/2016/09/13/technology/apple-coding-app-swift-playgrounds.html.

Smith, F. T. (2000). *Daubert and its progeny: Scientific Evidence in product liability litigation*. Washington, DC: Washington Legal Foundation.

Smith, M. (2014, November 29). End of Texas school's book ban doesn't mark the last chapter. *New York Times*. Retrieved from: http://www.nytimes.com/2014/11/30/us/end-of-schools-book-ban-doesnt-mark-the-last-chapter.html.

Snavely, B. (2016, July 1). Fiat Chrysler keeps astounding sales streak alive. *Detroit Free Press*. Retrieved from: http://www.freep.com/story/money/cars/chrysler/2016/07/01/fca-sales-pacifica-jeep-manley/86570954.

Snavely, B., & Gardner, G. (2016, July 26). FCA's astounding sales streak actually ended in 2013, after revision. *Detroit Free Press*. Retrieved from: http://www.freep.com/story/money/cars/chrysler/2016/07/26/fca-sales-streak-actually-ended-2013-chrysler/87570846.

Spencer, T. (2017, November 26). New Florida law expected to increase textbook challenges. *Washington Post*. Retrieved from: https://www.washingtonpost.com/national/new-florida-law-expected-to-increase-textbook-challenges/2017/11/26/c0f53470-d2b6-11e7-9ad9-ca0619edfa05_story.html.

Stack, L. (2016, February 12). Maryland University reinstates two faculty members amid outcry. *New York Times*. Retrieved from: https://www.nytimes.com/2016/02/13/us/maryland-university-reinstates-two-faculty-members-amid-outcry.html.

State Board of Education. (2017). Texas Education Agency. Author. Retrieved from: http://tea.texas.gov/sboe.

Steiner, D., & Vitti, N. (2016, October 27). Duval and high-quality curriculum: A conversation with Superintendent Nikolai Vitti. Institute for Education Policy. Retrieved from: http://edpolicy.education.jhu.edu/wordpress/?p=940.

Stevens, J. (2012, March 12). Heavy school bags are "deforming" children as growing numbers suffer irreversible back problems. *Daily Mail*. Retrieved from: http://www.dailymail.co.uk/news/article-2114118/Heavy-school-bags-deforming-children-growing-numbers-suffer-irreversible-problems.html.

Straumsheim, C. (2017, January 18). No more "Beall's List." *Inside Higher Ed*. Retrieved from: https://www.insidehighered.com/news/2017/01/18/librarians-list-predatory-journals-reportedly-removed-due-threats-and-politics.

Strauss, V. (2015, September 23). Common Core: "the gift that Pearson counts on to keep giving." *Washington Post*. Retrieved from: https://www.washingtonpost.com/news/answer-sheet/wp/2015/09/23/common-core-the-gift-that-pearson-counts-on-to-keep-giving.

Streiff, J. (2016, October 26). Donald Trump's earned media strategy bites him in his plump posterior. Redstate.com. Retrieved from: http://www.redstate.com/streiff/2016/10/26/donald-trumps-earned-media-strategy-bites-plump-posterior.

Sun Sentinel Editorial Board. (2017, January 27). Repeal ban of liquor in Florida grocery stores. *Sun-Sentinel*. Retrieved from: http://www.sun-sentinel.com/opinion/editorials/fl-editorial-liquor-regulations-20170127-story.html.

Svrluga, S. (2016, February 9). The controversy at Mount St. Mary's goes national after professors are fired. *Washington Post*. Retrieved from: https://www.washingtonpost.com/news/grade-point/wp/2016/02/09/the-controversy-at-mount-st-marys-goes-national-after-professors-are-fired.

Swier, R. (2014, May 3). Florida legislature passes two landmark bills: Textbooks and American laws for American courts. Teapartytribune.com. Retrieved from: http://www.teapartytribune.com/2014/05/03/florida-legislature-passes-two-landmark-bills-textbooks-and-american-laws-for-american-courts.

Swoger, B. (2012, September 26). Why are journals so expensive? *Scientific American*. Retrieved from: https://blogs.scientificamerican.com/information-culture/why-are-journals-so-expensive.

Tallahassee Democrat Editorial Board. (2017, February 4). "Liquor wall" a relic that needs to come down. *Tallahassee Democrat*. Retrieved from: http://www.tallahassee.com/story/opinion/editorials/2017/02/04/opinion-liquor-wall-relic-needs-come/97454852.

Tam, S. (2017, June 23). The Slants on the power of repurposing a slur. *New York Times*. Retrieved from: https://www.nytimes.com/2017/06/23/opinion/the-power-of-repurposing-a-slur.html.

Tara Parker-Pope, T. (2009, July 21). Weighing school backpacks. *New York Times*. Retrieved from: http://well.blogs.nytimes.com/2009/07/21/weighing-school-backpacks.

Taylor, K. (2014 December 10). New York State education commissioner to leave for federal post. *New York Times*. Retrieved from: https://www.nytimes.com/2014/12/11/nyregion/john-king-new-york-state-education-commissioner-is-leaving-for-federal-post.html.

Tear down Florida's "liquor wall." (2017, February 9). News-journalonline.com. Retrieved from: http://www.news-journalonline.com/opinion/20170209/our-view-tear-down-floridas-liquor-wall.

Texas Education Agency. (2017). Academics. Author. Retrieved from: http://tea.texas.gov/Academics.

Texas textbooks: What happened, what it means, and what we can do about it. (2010, June 18). Pfaw.org. Retrieved from: http://www.pfaw.org/rww-in-focus/texas-textbooks-what-happened-what-it-means-and-what-we-can-do-about-it.

Thevenot, B. (2010, March 26). The textbook myth. *Texas Tribune*. Retrieved from: https://www.texastribune.org/2010/03/26/texas-textbooks-national-influence-is-a-myth.

Thompson, C. (2017, October 8). Technology connects students, teachers in wake of hurricanes. *Florida Times-Union*. Retrieved from: http://digital.olivesoftware.com/Olive/ODN/FloridaTimesUnion/shared/ShowArticle.aspx?doc=TFTU%2F2017%2F10%2F08&entity=Ar05701&sk=D1B1A92A&mode=text.

Times Union believes pigs fly. (2015, June 24). Jaxkidsmatter.blogspot.com. Retrieved from: http://jaxkidsmatter.blogspot.com/2015/06/the-times-union-believes-pigs-fly.html.

Tomassini, J. (2012, May 8). Educators weigh e-textbook cost comparisons. *Education Week*. Retrieved from: http://www.edweek.org/ew/articles/2012/05/09/30etextbooks_ep.h31.html.

Toure, M. (2017, February 7). NYC high school students skip class to protest Trump. *Observer.com*. Retrieved from: http://observer.com/2017/02/nyc-high-school-students-skip-class-to-protest-trump.

Trex, E. (2011, September 2). Why are textbooks so expensive? Mentalfloss.com. Retrieved from: http://mentalfloss.com/article/28671/why-are-textbooks-so-expensive.

Trump on Twitter: Putin, Iran, Betsy DeVos. (2017, February 7). Reuters.com. Retrieved from: http://www.reuters.com/article/us-usa-trump-tweet-idUSKBN15M1IS.

Tuma, M. (2016, August 26). Texas State Board of Education. *Austin Chronicle*. Retrieved from: http://www.austinchronicle.com/news/2016-08-26/texas-state-board-of-education.

Turner, J. (2017, February 15). Changes in store for "liquor wall" plan. News4jax.com. Retrieved from: http://www.news4jax.com/news/changes-in-store-for-liquor-wall-plan.

Velderman. B. (2014, March 3). Does Jeb Bush realize Common Core threatens school choice concept? Foxnews.com. Retrieved from: http://www.foxnews.com/opinion/2014/03/03/does-jeb-bush-realize-common-core-threatens-school-choice-concept.html.

Vlasic, B., & Boudette, N. E. (2016, July 31). Why monthly auto sales numbers may not be what they seem. *New York Times*. Retrieved from: http://www.nytimes.com/2016/08/01/business/why-monthly-auto-sales-numbers-may-not-be-what-they-seem.html.

Walker, N. T., Bean, T. W., & Dillard, B. (2010). *When textbooks fall short: New ways, new texts, new sources of information in the content areas*. Portsmouth, NH: Heinemann.

Walker, T. (2016). Don't know much about history. National Education Association. Retrieved from: http://www.nea.org/home/39060.htm.

Wall Street Journal Editorial Board. (2015a, July 12). Teachers union votes Hillary. *Wall Street Journal*. Retrieved from: http://www.wsj.com/articles/the-teachers-union-votes-hillary-1436741319.

Wall Street Journal Editorial Board. (2015b, November 11). Clinton turns against charters. *Wall Street Journal*. Retrieved from: http://www.wsj.com/articles/clinton-turns-against-charters-1447287564.

Wall Street Journal Editorial Board. (2016a, March 18). Back to bad schools in the bayou. *Wall Street Journal*. Retrieved from: https://www.wsj.com/articles/back-to-bad-schools-in-the-bayou-1458342194.

Wall Street Journal Editorial Board. (2016b, October 16). The NAACP's disgrace. *Wall Street Journal*. Retrieved from: http://www.wsj.com/articles/the-naacps-disgrace-1476653537.

Wall Street Journal Editorial Board. (2016c, November 9). A school choice bonus. *Wall Street Journal*. Retrieved from: http://www.wsj.com/articles/a-school-choice-bonus-1478649927.

Wall Street Journal Editorial Board. (2017a, January 26). Chuck Schumer goes wild: The Democratic Senate leader loses his cool over Betsy DeVos. *Wall Street Journal*. Retrieved from: http://www.wsj.com/articles/chuck-schumer-goes-wild-1485477711.

Wall Street Journal Editorial Board. (2017b, January 29). Scott Walker's school bonus. *Wall Street Journal*. Retrieved from: https://www.wsj.com/articles/scott-walkers-school-bonus-1485735556.

Wall Street Journal Editorial Board. (2017c, January 30). The GOP's DeVos doubters. *Wall Street Journal*. Retrieved from: https://www.wsj.com/articles/the-gops-devos-doubters-1485822754.

Wall Street Journal Editorial Board. (2017d, February 2). Betsy DeVos's school frenemies. *Wall Street Journal*. Retrieved from: https://www.wsj.com/articles/betsy-devoss-school-frenemies-1486081958.

Wall Street Journal Editorial Board. (2017e, February 8). The real Democratic Party. *Wall Street Journal*. Retrieved from: https://www.wsj.com/articles/the-real-democratic-party-1486513439.

Wall Street Journal Editorial Board. (2017f, March 15). California's teacher tax break. *Wall Street Journal*. Retrieved from: https://www.wsj.com/articles/californias-teacher-tax-break-1489620659.

Wall Street Journal Editorial Board. (2017g, July 5). State of the teachers union. *Wall Street Journal*. Retrieved from: https://www.wsj.com/articles/state-of-the-teachers-union-1499297619.

Wall Street Journal Editorial Board. (2017h, July 13). The teachers no one wants. *Wall Street Journal*. Retrieved from: https://www.wsj.com/articles/the-teachers-no-one-wants-1499989012.

Wall Street Journal Editorial Board. (2017i, July 23). Randi Weingarten's "racism" rant. *Wall Street Journal*. Retrieved from: https://www.wsj.com/articles/randi-weingartens-racism-rant-1500845156.

Wall Street Journal Editorial Board. (2017j, August 22). New York attacks Success. *Wall Street Journal. Retrieved from:* https://www.wsj.com/articles/new-york-attacks-success-1503443366.

Wall Street Journal Editorial Board. (2018, April 17). Crowding out K-12 education. *Wall Street Journal*. Retrieved from: www.wsj.com/articles/crowding-out-k-12-education-1523921017.

Wallop, H. (2014, October 22). Why must my children's school bags be so heavy? *Daily Telegraph*. Retrieved from: http://www.telegraph.co.uk/men/relationships/fatherhood/11179065/Why-must-my-childrens-school-bags-be-so-heavy.html.

Washington Redskins: Offensive? And who decides? (2016, May 20). *New York Times*. Retrieved from: http://nyti.ms/1rZfaYC.

Weissert, W. (2014, November 21). Texas approves disputed history texts for schools. *San Diego Union-Tribune*. Retrieved from: http://www.sandiegouniontribune.com/sdut-publisher-withdraws-textbook-up-for-texas-approval-2014nov21-story.html.

West, L. (2015, November 15). Political correctness' doesn't hinder free speech—It expands it. *New York Times*. Retrieved from: https://www.theguardian.com/commentisfree/2015/nov/15/political-correctness-free-speech-racism-misogyny-university-yale-missouri.

Why textbooks are important. (2009, June 19). Wordpress.com. Retrieved from: https://tapbb.wordpress.com/2009/06/19/why-textbooks-are-important.

Wray, D. (2015, July 9). 5 Reasons the new Texas social studies textbooks are nuts. *Houstonpress.com*. Retrieved from: http://www.houstonpress.com/news/5-reasons-the-new-texas-social-studies-textbooks-are-nuts-7573825.

Wright, S. (2015, November 17). Can political correctness and free speech coexist on campus? Abovethelaw.com. Retrieved from: http://abovethelaw.com/2015/11/can-political-correctness-and-free-speech-coexist-on-campus.

Yudkevich, M. (2012, March 18). Publications for money: What creates the market for paid academic journals? *Inside Higher Ed*. Retrieved from: https://www.insidehighered.com/blogs/world-view/publications-money-what-creates-market-paid-academic-journals.

Zekaria, S. (2015, February 27). Pearson confident of bright future after completing restructuring plan. *Wall Street Journal*. Retrieved from: http://www.politico.com/story/2015/02/pearson-education-115026.

Zekaria, S. (2016, January 21). Pearson to cut 10% of workforce as it issues profit warning. *Wall Street Journal*. Retrieved from: http://www.wsj.com/articles/pearson-to-cut-10-of-workforce-as-it-issues-profit-warning-1453367509.

Zernike, K. (2016, November 23). Steered money from public schools. *New York Times*. Retrieved from: http://www.nytimes.com/2016/11/23/us/politics/betsy-devos-trumps-education-pick-has-steered-money-from-public-schools.html.

Zwaagstra, M. (2014, February 22). Textbooks are still important. *Winnipeg Free Press*. Retrieved from: http://www.winnipegfreepress.com/opinion/analysis/Textbooks-are-still-important-246719221.html.

About the Author

Gerard Giordano is professor at the University of North Florida and has written more than a dozen books about education. He has published a recent series with Rowman & Littlefield about the questions parents have raised about their children's schools.

www.ingramcontent.com/pod-product-compliance
Lightning Source LLC
Chambersburg PA
CBHW030117010526
44116CB00005B/284